EXPLORING ENVIRONMENTAL ISSUES

Glencoe Science Professional Series

McGraw-Hill

New York, New York   Columbus, Ohio   Mission Hills, California   Peoria, Illinois

Contributing Author: Barbara Branca

Send all inquiries to:

Glencoe/McGraw-Hill
936 Eastwind Drive
Westerville, OH 43081

Printed in the United States of America.

ISBN 0-02-826312-X

7 8 9 10 11 12 13 14   066   05 04 03 02 01 00 99 98 97

Contents

To the Teacher 4T

Teacher's Notes 5T

Activity

1 Water, Water, Everywhere? 1

2 Sources of Water Pollution 3

3 The Air We Breathe 5

4 Is It Getting Hot in Here? 7

5 Save Our Skins: Ozone Depletion
and Skin Disorders 9

6 Toxic Waste—Where Does It Go? 11

7 Organically Grown 13

8 Hold On To That Soil 15

9 Energy: Renewable or Nonrenewable 17

10 What's Your Energy Quotient? 19

11 How Many Is a Crowd? 23

12 Using Land Wisely 25

13 Sorting It Out with Recycling 27

14 Going, Going, Gone: Endangerment
and Extinction 31

15 Sharing the World with Wildlife 33

16 Thank a Tree 37

17 The Rain Forest 39

18 Why Are Wetlands Important? 41

19 Balancing Act 43

20 Be an Earthwise Consumer 47

Exploring Environmental Issues gives students the opportunity to examine the changes produced in the environment largely as a result of human activity. Among the issues considered are water and air pollution, global warming, ozone depletion, toxic waste, soil erosion, resource depletion, pest control, habitat destruction, and species endangerment. As responsible future citizens, students are encouraged to think about whether pollution and other forms of environmental deterioration are the inevitable results of growing populations and industrialization, or if there are individual choices and group initiatives that can solve or at least mitigate these problems.

One of the major unifying themes of biology is the concept of interrelationships among organisms—interrelationships with each other and with the physical environment. Thus, *Exploring Environmental Issues* is designed to be used in conjunction with a general biology course to help awaken the student's environmental consciousness and extend understanding of the interdependence and diversity of life on Earth. The teaching notes included at the front of this booklet offer suggestions for correlating each student activity with basic topics in the biology course, but you may choose to use the material in other ways, depending on the interests and abilities of your students.

Each of the twenty student activities begins with a section called *The Big Picture* which presents necessary background information and vocabulary, and it discusses significant issues of the topic. Then, in the *Just Do It* section, students are given the opportunity to work on projects that may involve observation and data collection in their local area, or that may require research to assess the scope of problems on national and global levels. Many of these projects are appropriate for cooperative group work. Next, in the *Decision Making* section, students analyze and interpret their information and apply their knowledge to other related questions. Finally, the *Going Further* section suggests other high-interest projects for students in and out of the classroom.

For each activity, the teaching notes include additional background information and related readings, suggestions of government agencies or other sources of useful materials, procedural steps to help students complete the activity, possible outcomes or answers, and other options for extending the study.

PURPOSE
This lesson focuses on the resource of fresh water. Students will learn about the water cycle, become familiar with the source of their drinking water, and discuss methods of conservation.

BACKGROUND
Water sources vary widely from municipal systems that pipe water from distant reservoirs and treat it for use by millions of users, to individual wells that tap into the water table close to home.

READINGS
Water Fit to Drink by Carol Keough (Rodale Press, Emmaus, PA, 1980) offers very complete coverage of water systems and water quality.

MATERIALS AND METHODS
To help students locate the source of their drinking water, have on hand phone numbers and addresses of the municipal water supplier, private well companies, or well drillers in your area. Provide regional maps that will guide students as they attempt to draw a map showing the watershed. Information about local rock structure and aquifers may be available at public or university libraries, from the municipal agency in charge of water supply, or from the U.S. Geological Survey. Check also any environmental impact statements done for development in your area. Data about current reservoir levels may be included on the weather page of the local newspaper.

TEACHING STRATEGIES
Possible subjects to correlate with this lesson include the need for water by all living things, cell metabolism and cell processes, human body systems, health and control of disease, pollution and the environment.

POSSIBLE OUTCOMES
Just Do It: 1. Students may find that their water comes from diverse sources—from a municipal source which may be filtered, aerated, and chlorinated to a private well that draws untreated water up from hundreds of feet below ground. **6.** Students may be surprised to find out that they may be personally using over 50 gallons of water a day.

Decision Making: 1. Students should ask for detailed descriptions of the kind of products to be manufactured in the proposed factory, the raw materials that would be involved in the manufacturing process, and the by-products of manufacture. **2.** Students may suggest conservation techniques that include taking shorter showers or cutting down on running water while they wash dishes or brush their teeth.

EXTENSIONS
Contact your local historical society for information about the historical importance of the area's waterways. Encourage students to increase their awareness of water use through poster campaigns or other awareness activities.

SOURCES OF WATER POLLUTION   ACTIVITY 2

PURPOSE
This lesson focuses on the variety of contaminants that may be present in the water supply, where they come from, and what risks they pose. Students research which pollutants are tested for in their local water supply and compare their results to EPA standards.

BACKGROUND
The Environmental Protection Agency (EPA) recognizes approximately one thousand toxins in water and there may be at least as many not recognized by that agency.

READINGS
For a complete listing of potential toxins in water, read *Earthright*, by H. Patricia Hynes (Prima Publishing & Communication, PO Box 1260PH, Rocklin, CA 95677).

MATERIALS AND METHODS
Help students locate and decipher local water test results. You may wish to call the EPA Safe Drinking Water Hotline at 1-(800) 426-4791 for a list of regulated contaminants and guidelines.

TEACHING STRATEGIES
Possible subjects to correlate with this lesson are human physiology, cell metabolism, health and disease control, aquatic ecosystems, pollution, and the environment.

POSSIBLE OUTCOMES
Just Do It: 3. Students may be alarmed by the list of toxins that can be present in their drinking water. They may find that their water supplies (or source of water) meet all the standards that were set by EPA for certain pollutants, but that there may be many other chemicals in the water for which tests were not run. Students may wish to learn more about how EPA standards are established and to evaluate the level of safety being set.

Decision Making: 2. Point out that some home water filtration systems bear negative side-effects such as the addition of sodium to the water which may be unhealthful for some individuals and the removal of trace elements that may be beneficial to others. **3.** Students may suggest replacing lawns with decorative stone or wood chips.

EXTENSIONS
Plan a visit to your local water treatment plant. Invite a water purification expert or an expert on the pollution of local waterways to come to class.

PURPOSE

This lesson focuses on sources and types of air pollutants. Students analyze the air quality in their immediate environment according to several criteria.

BACKGROUND

Because of enforcement of the many air quality laws, industry emissions of carbon dioxide, carbon monoxide, and sulfur dioxide have been greatly reduced. However, there are still fine particles of pollutants in the air as a result of the burning of fossil fuels. Studies have revealed that long-term exposure to such small particles can raise the risk of early death from heart or lung disease.

READINGS

Our Earth, Ourselves, The Action-Oriented Guide to Help You Protect and Preserve Our Environment by Ruth Caplan, Executive Director of Environmental Action (Philip Lief Group Book, Bantam, 1990) is a practical source of information about air quality.

MATERIALS AND METHODS

For assessing outdoor pollution, check with local officials about the source and extent of smog in your area. To check for particulates, students will need only small amounts of petroleum jelly. For sources of indoor pollution monitoring devices, first try local hardware and houseware stores. For more information about a complete check-up of a building, a good source is *House Dangerous: Indoor Pollution in Your Home and Office — and What You Can Do About It!* by Ellen J. Greenfield (Vintage Books, Random House, 1987).

TEACHING STRATEGIES

Possible subjects to correlate include the human respiratory system, respiratory diseases and the immune response, the process of gas exchange across membranes in plants and animals, abiotic factors in the ecosystem, and air quality in the environment.

POSSIBLE OUTCOMES

Just Do It: Students will have a range of results expressed by the number of checks they make. They will find that the problems indicated by some of the checks are not under their control. Smog problems affect an entire region, whereas visible particulate air pollution is restricted to areas close to incineration. If there is incineration nearby, visible soot will cling to the surface of the petroleum jelly. The presence of carbon monoxide, cigarette smoke, formaldehyde, and asbestos will vary from house to house.

Decision Making: 1. Students may think of changing some of the conditions over which they or the adults with whom they live have control: living in a smoke free environment, purchasing new household items with concern for formaldehyde, testing for radon and asbestos, installing vents for stoves. For problems that stem from outside the home, they may think of contacting the regional EPA office to report excessive air pollution. **2.** Students may suggest writing legislators about the urgency of enforcing air quality laws. **3.** Students should discuss the ethical issues of selling pollution allowances and how it affects air pollution in other areas.

EXTENSIONS

Ask students to research the progress in the development of alternative automobile fuels such as ethanol, hydrogen, and methanol or the use of electric cars.

IS IT GETTING HOT IN HERE? ACTIVITY 4

PURPOSE

This lesson explains the greenhouse effect and discusses the possible causes of global warming. Students graph and analyze data about greenhouse gases. They use data to predict and hypothesize about future climate conditions.

BACKGROUND

The greenhouse effect keeps Earth at a temperature hospitable to life. However, human activity causes increases in the atmospheric content of greenhouse gases and, thereby, may be increasing the greenhouse effect and altering global climate.

READINGS

Hothouse Earth, the Greenhouse Effect and Gaia, by John Gribbin (Grove Weidenfeld, NY, 1990) tracks actual data of CO_2 concentrations of the atmosphere recorded at Mauna Loa from late 1950s to 1988 and explains climate changes on Earth over time, scientific models of cycles, and the Gaia hypothesis—that Earth is a living organism.

MATERIALS AND METHODS

Students will need graph paper and construction paper to display their graphs. If possible, use graphics software and have students make graphs on computers.

TEACHING STRATEGIES

Possible subjects to correlate with this lesson include photosynthesis, gas exchange in living things, energy within cells, abiotic factors of the environment, ecosystems, and human activity and the environment.

POSSIBLE OUTCOMES

Just Do It: 1. Student graphs will show that CO_2 is the predominant greenhouse gas and that its content in the atmosphere has increased sharply over the last few decades. **2a.** The rate at which CO_2 increased from 1860 to 1880 was 0.1 ppm per year. **2b.** In the decade 1980 to 1990, the increase was 1.5 ppm per year. **2c.** If 1990 statistics show 350 ppm of CO_2 and if the rate of increase is 2 ppm per year, the content in 2000 will be 370 ppm. **3.** Average temperatures will differ by region. Student scenarios may include changes in the coastline due to flooding, changes in the life cycles of plants and animals, and changes in the progression of the seasons.

Decision Making: 1. Students may want to show how

their country is planning to reduce CO_2 emissions. **2.** Tree planting along highways to reduce CO_2 has been done in many locations. Scientists do not agree about how old the trees must be to have a significant effect.

EXTENSIONS
For more information about global warming and other topics write for a free environmental education packet available from the Environmental Defense Fund, 257 Park Avenue South, New York, NY 10010, 1-(212) 505-2100.

SAVE OUR SKINS: OZONE DEPLETION AND SKIN DISORDERS   ACTIVITY 5

PURPOSE
This lesson focuses on the causes and effects of ozone depletion. Students calculate how much the ozone hole over Antarctica has increased in size during a ten-year period and take a survey of sun protection products available.

BACKGROUND
One proposed cause of ozone thinning is by compounds known as chlorofluorocarbons or CFCs. As early as 1975, Johnson Wax, the first of several manufacturers, ceased production of CFCs. However, global participation in banning all compounds that deplete the ozone has yet to occur and the ozone hole over Antarctica has grown considerably over the last decade.

READINGS
Ozone Crisis: The 15-year Evolution of a Sudden Global Emergency by Sharon Roan (Wiley, 1989), chronicles the story of the scientists who first discovered the ozone hole and gives a history of scientific and governmental action since. *Ozone*, by Kathlyn Gay (Franklin Watts, 1989), is another easy-to-read account of the ozone shield.

MATERIALS AND METHODS
For measuring the size of the ozone hole, students should trace the hole onto graph paper. Paper with 20 squares per inch makes the calculation more accurate. Have students count the number of squares covered by the hole in 1982 and then in 1992. To compare the two numbers, students may use an equation like this one where N is the number of squares:

$$\% \text{ increase} = \frac{N_2 - N_1}{N_1} \times 100$$

TEACHING STRATEGIES
Possible subjects to correlate with this lesson include structure and function of the cell and its organelles, human immune system, the skin and the sense organs, and humans and the environment.

POSSIBLE OUTCOMES
Just Do It: 1b. Students may calculate a 75% to 80% increase in the size of the ozone hole. **2.** Although climate varies regionally, students will probably hypothesize that they should wear sunscreen from late spring through the summer and fall. If they spend a great deal of time outside during winter months, especially under sunny conditions where there is reflective snow on the ground, they should wear it all year long. **3.** In their survey of sun protection products they will probably find a growing assortment of products with an SPF greater than 15, perhaps as great as 45. SPF stands for Sun Protection Factor and it represents how many times longer you can stay in the sun before burning than you can with no sunscreen protection. **4.** Students may find that sunglasses with UVB protection may be more expensive.

Decision Making: 1. Encourage students to discuss among their friends the harmful effects caused by exposure to the sun on the skin and eyes. **2.** Halons contribute to ozone depletion and students may suggest that they would purchase the alternative. **4.** If the only product to be found contains CFCs, students may suggest that they would go without.

EXTENSIONS
Contact a local business person from an appliance store or car repair shop who can visit the class and discuss how CFCs are captured.

TOXIC WASTE—WHERE DOES IT GO?   ACTIVITY 6

PURPOSE
This lesson focuses on amounts, variety, and hazards of toxic waste. Students take a survey of possible toxins that they have at home.

BACKGROUND
Toxic waste refers to the thousands of potentially dangerous chemicals that are disposed of daily and can get into the soil and water. Some of the chemicals found in the home can also be dangerous.

READINGS

Save Our Planet: 750 Everyday Ways You Can Help Clean Up the Earth by Diane MacEachern (Dell, 1990) is packed with good information and a variety of activities on all topics of environmental concern. Another helpful source is *Design for a Livable Planet: How You Can Help Clean Up the Environment* by Jon Naar (Harper & Row, 1990) which also contains information on energy conservation and recycling.

MATERIALS AND METHODS

Encourage students to take the survey home and write down the toxins they have observed. If possible, get approval for student access to the school building to see what possible toxins exist there.

TEACHING STRATEGIES

Possible subjects to correlate include the human nervous system including the senses, the respiratory system and its disorders, ecosystems, or pollution and the environment.

POSSIBLE OUTCOMES

Just Do It: Students are likely to find at least some of the toxins listed in their homes.

Decision Making: 1. *Save Our Planet* (mentioned above) contains many practical nonpolluting alternatives. Some of the cleaning agents that can be substituted are washing soda and borax solutions instead of chemical cleaners. Students may suggest that alternatives are nonpolluting but may not work as well. **2.** New products on the market do show a response to growing consumer awareness of environmental issues. **3.** To find out if there is a Superfund site near you, contact your local EPA office. **4.** Your town recycling center may accept motor oil.

EXTENSIONS

To encourage students to write inquiry letters about suspected toxic dumping, send for a copy of "Freedom of Information Act: A User's Guide," Freedom of Information Clearinghouse, PO Box 19367, Washington, D.C., 20036.

ORGANICALLY GROWN   ACTIVITY 7

PURPOSE

This lesson focuses on organic farming methods and the possible benefits. Students construct a compost bin and observe the effects of using compost on growing plants.

BACKGROUND

Growing food organically means using natural pest controls rather than applying chemical pesticides and building up the soil by rotating crops and recycling organic wastes rather than applying chemical fertilizers. The persistent use of chemicals in growing and processing food has been linked to a variety of human ailments.

READINGS

For a listing of the quantities of pesticides in fruits and vegetables, read "Intolerable Risk: Pesticides in Our Children's Food, A Report" by the Natural Resources Defense Council, February 1989 or *Pesticide Alert: A Guide to Pesticides in Fruits and Vegetables* by L. Mott and K. Snyder (Sierra Club Books, 1988).

MATERIALS AND METHODS

Work with technology, art, or industrial arts teachers in your school to get scrap lumber, chicken wire, or even cinder blocks to make the compost bins. Local businesses may be willing to donate these materials also.

TEACHING STRATEGIES

Possible subjects to correlate with this lesson include reproduction and development in animals, nutrition, digestion, the nitrogen cycle, the process of organic decay, and ecosystems.

POSSIBLE OUTCOMES

Just Do It: Modify the recipe for compost to suit your situation. Covering compost with black plastic retains heat and moisture while preventing the unwanted growth of plants.

Decision Making: 1. Students may suggest that compost-fed plants grow fuller and have more blooms and fruit. **2.** An organic fruit usually looks less perfect, with uneven color and spots on the skin, but the main advantage is that it contains no chemicals. **3.** Students may suggest some limits for chemical residues should be established based on the body weight of children, not adults. **4.** Encourage debate over whether or not weed killers on lawns should be restricted.

EXTENSIONS

Ask an organic farmer or Integrated Pest Management expert to visit the class. If facilities are available, encourage students to experiment with growing plants with and without chemical controls. Consult back issues of *Organic Gardening* magazine for helpful tips.

HOLD ON TO THAT SOIL   ACTIVITY 8

PURPOSE

This lesson focuses on the importance of soil and discusses activities that lead to soil loss. Students will examine soil samples, construct a soil profile, design a demonstration to show soil erosion, and apply what they have learned to identify areas sensitive to erosion in their community.

BACKGROUND

The soil is an important abiotic factor in any ecosystem, often limiting which plants will grow there. Soil is an important natural resource which must be protected, and the problems of soil depletion and erosion must be addressed in any conservation program.

MATERIALS AND METHODS

For digging soil samples, use shovels or hand trowels. Ask students to bring in plastic containers to hold the soil taken from outdoors. You will need paper towels and hand lenses to examine the soil. Before the class digs for samples, find a suitable spot as cultivated areas with added topsoil may not be indicative of soil type. Locate an out-of-the way place where digging will not disturb vegetation, especially tree roots. Digging deep holes is impractical and it is suggested that for examining the soil profile you scout around for road cuts or construction sites that are fairly deep and will expose subsoil layers. For the erosion demonstrations ask students to bring pie pans and trays from home or use cafeteria trays if possible. Encourage students to improvise and to make their own watering cans, sloping surfaces, and so on. Geology books and even an encyclopedia will show a soil map of the United States.

TEACHING STRATEGIES

Possible subjects to correlate include the needs of plants, transport in plants, abiotic factors in an ecosystem, the process of decay and decomposition of organic matter, and biomes of the world.

POSSIBLE OUTCOMES

Just Do It: Students may find a variety of soil textures determined by particle size. Sands are the largest particles and easily seen, usually made of quartz, gypsum, or calcite. Silts are just large enough to be seen and are composed of weathered sedimentary rocks. Clays are microscopic particles made of weathered feldspar and other minerals. Soils known as loam contain sand, silt, and clay. Consult a geology book for photographs of each type. Soil types around the country vary. In general, the Northeast contains forest soils with a brownish-gray topsoil layer rich in humus, underlain by sandy soil. The southeastern forest soils appear more red to yellow because of the higher clay content. The central part of the country has rich loamy prairie soil. The mountain soils found throughout the American West have a relatively thin topsoil layer that contains particles of rock still in the process of mechanical weathering. The southwestern desert soils are made of mostly sand and weathered minerals.

Decision Making: 1. Students are likely to give examples of fences, walls, earthen mounds, and plantings used to prevent erosion. **2.** A proposal should state the observed erosion, and cite examples of how this proposed solution has worked in similar situations. **3.** Maps of soil use can be found in geology texts and environmental impact statements. **4.** Encourage a discussion of RVs and trail bikes, making sure that students are aware of how overuse of trails can erode the land.

EXTENSIONS

Contact the local office of the Soil Conservation Service (part of the Department of Agriculture), or your county soil and water conservation district for a speaker who can discuss soil types and test your soil. In urban locations, consider taking a field trip to a city park in which the natural topography can be better observed.

ENERGY: RENEWABLE AND NONRENEWABLE   ACTIVITY 9

PURPOSE

This lesson focuses on the need for renewable and nonpolluting energy sources. Students construct and use a solar cooker and hot water heater.

BACKGROUND

Although most people get electric energy through the burning of fossil fuels, a nonrenewable resource, there are some alternatives that use renewable sources including solar, wind, and geothermal energy.

READINGS

How to Solarize Your House, by Thomas Scott Dean and Jay W. Hedden (Scribner's, 1980) includes maps showing the mean solar radiation and temperatures of the United States month by month. *Saving the Planet: How to Shape an Environmentally Sustainable Global Economy* by Lester R. Brown, Christopher Flavin and Sandra Postel (Worldwatch Institute, 1991) takes a global view of building a solar economy.

MATERIALS AND METHODS

Help students gather materials they may need including aluminum foil, wood, glass, insulating material, and black paint. Helpful magazines that show how to design solar devices include back issues of *Popular Science*, *New Shelter*, and *Solar Age*.

TEACHING STRATEGIES

Possible subjects to correlate include matter and energy of living things, energy changes in the cell, the flow of energy in the ecosystem, and humans and the environment.

POSSIBLE OUTCOMES

Just Do It: Encourage students to come up with their own version of solar designs found in books or magazines.

Decision Making: 1. Solar technology, especially for passive solar design, is available in all parts of the country, even where the weather is cold and cloudy. **2.** Power generation by wind on a large scale is limited to places where the wind blows steadily. However, in rural areas, a single-unit wind turbine generates up to 10 kilowatts, enough power for an average household. **3.** Alternative energy sources vary from region to region. Student answers might suggest that the government should spend money to construct alternative energy plants if a technology is feasible in that region.

EXTENSIONS

Encourage interested students to explore the possibility of making a wind generator. To receive a free publications list and fact sheets on renewable energy technologies, contact the Conservation and Renewable Energy Inquiry and Referral Service, or CAREIRS, (auspices of the Department of Energy), PO Box 3048, Merrifield, VA 22116, 1-(800) 523-2929.

WHAT'S YOUR ENERGY QUOTIENT?   ACTIVITY 10

PURPOSE

This lesson focuses on current levels of energy usage in the United States and discusses energy conservation measures. Students take an energy survey of their home and school in order to see how efficiently energy is used.

BACKGROUND

There is a great demand for electrical energy in the United States. Energy used for home heating, lighting, and appliances can be conserved if consumers use efficient equipment and practice conservation techniques. Local utilities usually publish guides showing how much energy various appliances use and offering conservation tips.

MATERIALS AND METHODS

Obtain any needed permissions to conduct an energy survey at school and be sensitive to the living situations of students for whom a school audit would be more appropriate. Make copies of the survey as needed.

TEACHING STRATEGIES

Possible subjects to correlate include matter and energy of living things, energy changes in the cell, the flow of energy in the ecosystem, warm-bloodedness in mammals, and humans and the environment.

POSSIBLE OUTCOMES

Just Do It: Students may show a wide range of energy quotients.

Decision Making: 1. Students may find they share some of the same negative responses. They may suggest specific energy conservation techniques, or they may suggest speaking to their parents or other adults about installing energy saving devices in the home.
2. Encourage students to share their results and find the average energy quotient. One way of rating the scores: 25 to 30 is excellent, 20 to 25 good, and below 20 is poor. **4.** The energy use increased from one winter to the next, perhaps because the second winter was colder and more heat was probably needed. Usage was greater the second summer because it was hotter and more air conditioning or fans may have been used. This customer shows above average use in the winter, perhaps because of an inefficient heating system or the use of electric heaters. In summer this customer showed below average use, perhaps because of an efficient cooling system.

EXTENSIONS

Make arrangements to show students how to read an electric meter in your school building. To learn more about energy efficiency, write to or call the American Council for an Energy Efficient Economy, Suite 535, 1001 Connecticut Avenue, NW, Washington, DC 20036, 1-(202) 429-8873.

HOW MANY IS A CROWD?   ACTIVITY 11

PURPOSE

This lesson focuses on population growth and quality of life issues. Students use statistical population data to make graphs, interpret them, and make predictions.

BACKGROUND

As explained in the opening paragraphs of the activity, the expanding human population has many effects on the limited resources on the planet.

READINGS

Saving the Planet: How to Shape an Environmentally Sustainable Global Economy by Lester R. Brown, Christopher Flavin, and Sandra Postel (Worldwatch Institute, 1991), offers much information about moving

toward a stable world population. *Healing the Planet, Strategies for Resolving the Environmental Crisis* by Paul and Anne Ehrlich (Addison-Wesley Publishing Co., 1991) has an emphasis on global population as do other books by Paul and Anne Ehrlich.

MATERIALS AND METHODS

Contact your board of education and ask them to share with you the census information they have gathered about your school district.

TEACHING STRATEGIES

Possible subjects to correlate include reproduction in animals, biotic factors in the environment, and population biology.

POSSIBLE OUTCOMES

Just Do It: Students should be able to use the population data you have provided to make a population bar graph showing number of people for each age or age group. Calculators will be useful for finding the average age and mode.

Decision Making: 1. Check school district figures for expected future enrollment. **2.** If your community is growing quickly it may become crowded and impact on the quality of life educationally, socially, economically, and culturally. **3.** This increase in population will probably lead to a decrease in the habitat area for plants and animals. **4.** There may be limiting factors like geological barriers to growth such as a river, mountain, or coast. Other limiting factors may be housing availability, job opportunities, and so on.

EXTENSIONS

Encourage creative students to write short science fiction stories using the premise of an overpopulated planet. For a free packet of educational materials on overpopulation, contact Zero Population Growth, 1400 16th Street, NW, Suite 320, Washington, DC 20036, 1-(202) 332-2200.

USING LAND WISELY   ACTIVITY 12

PURPOSE

This lesson focuses on the issue of balancing land development with preservation. Students interview someone who has lived in their community for a long time, collect data, and create a presentation that compares land use of the past with the present.

BACKGROUND

As the human population has grown in the technological age, more land is required for cities and towns, and with it increases in agriculture, manufacturing and commerce, activities which can deplete natural resources. Plans for future development must include maintaining a balance between preserving the natural environment with the needs of the human population.

MATERIALS AND METHODS

Contact senior citizen organizations, residential homes, and the local chapter of AARP for potential contacts for interviews. Approve the lists of questions prepared by students and the arrangements made with the interviewee before students go on the interview. For student presentations, have on hand maps of your area that can help students determine past and current land use.

TEACHING STRATEGIES

Possible subjects to correlate with this lesson include the needs of living things, population biology, renewable and nonrenewable resources, pollution in the environment, conservation, and resource management.

POSSIBLE OUTCOMES

Just Do It: Encourage creativity for student presentations that may range from a collage of memorabilia, a video of the interview, or a detailed map of the region.

Decision Making: 1. Answers will vary but students should gain some insight as to whether or not their community is growing rapidly, if housing will be increasing, and if the open spaces will be diminishing. **2.** Students should use their knowledge to make an intelligent appraisal of such a proposal and be able to pinpoint several alternative sites for such development in order to maintain established parks or open spaces. **3.** This scenario is not uncommon and raises the issue of compromise that often occurs between developers and environmentalists. Students may bring up the valid point that a road will disturb the area and shrink the habitat of animals in the preserve. Some may suggest that cutting timber adjacent to the preserved land already diminishes the range of wildlife. However, if there are areas nearby that are being disturbed by the excessive air pollution caused by trucks, there may be a good reason to cut a shorter road. **4.** Students may have their own emotional opinions about hunting, however, limited hunting in a preserve is often done to maintain the health of the existing herd. Without some thinning of the herd, a growing deer population will denude every bush and tree, including endangered plants, and still some deer will starve to death. **5.** As it implies, "mixed use" of land means that a parcel can be designated for more than one use such as some limited agriculture teamed with some recreational use.

EXTENSIONS

Contact you local Landmarks Commission or Historical Society and have a guest speaker come to your class. To find out more about the national park system, contact the Department of the Interior, National Park Service, Office of Public Inquiries, 1849 C Street, NW, Room 1013, Washington, DC 20240, 1-(202) 208-4747.

SORTING IT OUT WITH RECYCLING   ACTIVITY 13

PURPOSE

This lesson focuses on the problem of solid waste management. Students take a waste audit of their home, calculate what portion of their trash is recyclable, and learn more about recycling programs.

BACKGROUND

Recycling such materials as metals, plastics, glass, and paper reduces the need for new materials and directly prevents pollution and the loss of natural resources.

READINGS

For some very practical home hints for recycling and reducing trash, read *Heloise: Hints for a Healthy Planet*, Perigree Books (Putnam, 1990).

MATERIALS AND METHODS

Students need paper bags, scales and cartons, boxes, or storage crates to collect trash.

TEACHING STRATEGIES

Possible subjects to correlate include conservation and management of natural resources, pollution in the environment, and the process of decomposition.

POSSIBLE OUTCOMES

Just Do It: Students should carry out their garbage inventory for a week. If possible, plan a classroom activity for the same time period to maintain student interest and enthusiasm; for example: set up a paper recycling corner and find alternative uses for paper that is usually thrown away in the classroom.

Decision Making 1. Students should find out if there are existing or planned recycling programs. **2.** Students will find that certain trash items, especially plastic, take up volume in a landfill but do not necessarily weigh much. Challenge students to devise an alternative method for measuring trash by volume. **3.** Inquire about the volume of trash generated by the school cafeteria to help students discuss this question.

EXTENSIONS

Encourage students to set up a recycling center in your school, make useful items out of recycled materials, and experiment to compare how biodegradable some different materials are. To find out more about programs such as the Solid Waste Alternatives Project, contact the Environmental Action Foundation, 6930 Carroll Avenue, Suite 600, Takoma Park, MD 20912, 1-(301) 891-1100 for a list of available educational material and a copy of their quarterly magazine.

GOING, GOING, GONE: ENDANGERMENT AND EXTINCTION   ACTIVITY 14

PURPOSE

This lesson focuses on biodiversity and the global problem of habitat destruction. Students assess the number of endangered species, hypothesize the reasons for their endangerment, and analyze the effect of human activity on habitats.

BACKGROUND

Populations of many wild species, both animals and plants, have been decreasing often as a result of human activities. Changes in habitats due to agriculture or development occur so quickly that species are unable to adapt. Thus, even though extinction is a natural process, the rate of extinction of wildlife today has been greatly accelerated.

READINGS

Who's Endangered on Noah's Ark? Literary and Scientific Activities for Teachers and Parents by Glenn McGlathery and Norma J. Livo of the University of Colorado at Denver (Teacher Ideas Press, a division of Libraries Unlimited, Inc., Englewood, CO, 1992) features a discussion of extinction and endangerment, folklore, stories, and activities.

MATERIALS AND METHODS

Students need the list provided in the activity and any other information you have about endangered species in your state.

TEACHING STRATEGIES

Possible subjects to correlate with this lesson include evolution of species, classification of plants and animals, plant and animal adaptations and habitats, ecosystems, resources, and conservation.

POSSIBLE OUTCOMES

Just Do It: 1. The states with the greatest number of endangered species are Hawaii with 126 and California with 110. Hawaii has many unique species on each of its islands which are threatened by development of the limited land resources by a growing population. California is a very large state in area, encompassing many types of habitats from the redwood forest to the desert. It has many diverse species but also has the largest human population. The state with the smallest number of endangered species is Alaska with 6. Alaska is still considered a wilderness with its vast area and relatively low human population. The states of New Hampshire, Vermont, Maine, North Dakota, and South Dakota also have relatively low numbers of endangered species perhaps because these states have relatively small, established populations with conservation programs in place. **2.** Answers will vary by state. Contact your local conservation department or bureau of Fish and Wildlife to find out what endangered species are in your state. **3.** A conservation biologist in your area will be able to discuss the habitat in which endangered species live and programs in place to preserve that habitat.

Decision Making: 1. Students may suggest that taking animals from their habitat involves being responsible for those animals for perhaps generations until they can be returned to the wild. Individual animals may not thrive in captivity and there is no guarantee that the program will work, although there has been success for numerous species. **2.** Direct students to the library to find out more information in periodicals about this issue.

EXTENSIONS
For more information about endangered species, have students write to the U.S. Fish and Wildlife Service, Publications Unit, 130 Webb Building, 4401 N. Fairfax Drive, Arlington, VA 22203.

PURPOSE
This lesson focuses on ways in which humans and animal populations can coexist. Students research both the scientific facts and cultural significance of one animal, then synthesize what they have learned to create an original presentation in an artistic medium.

BACKGROUND
In addition to scientific study, much can be learned about animals by exploring native folklore, myths, stories, art, music, and literature from many cultures. This cultural perspective enriches our knowledge of wildlife management, the aim of which is to strike a delicate balance that meets the needs of both human and animal populations.

READINGS
Keepers of the Animals: Native American Stories and Wildlife Activities for Children by Michael J. Caduto and Joseph Bruchac (Fulcrum Publishing, Golden, CO, 1991) contains stories, activities, teaching techniques and field trips for wildlife. By the same authors written in 1989, there is *Keepers of the Earth: Native American Stories and Environmental Activities for Children*.

MATERIALS AND METHODS
Gather many references for students. As students choose their projects, they may require vastly different materials. Work cooperatively with teachers of other disciplines to gather appropriate art or music supplies and make this project a creative, open-ended one.

TEACHING STRATEGIES
Possible subjects to correlate with this lesson include the classification of animals, characteristics of vertebrates, animal adaptations, habitat and niches in the ecosystem, and conservation of resources.

POSSIBLE OUTCOMES
Just Do It: Student presentations will vary widely and give students who excel in areas other than science an opportunity to present their ideas with literature, art, craft, music, or film.

Decision Making: 1. Answers will vary. **2.** Keeping exotic pets without proper authorization and care may not only be ethically wrong, it may be illegal. **3.** If you find an injured animal you should contact a licensed animal rehabilitator and not try to nurse the animal back to health yourself.

EXTENSIONS
Contact a wildlife rehabilitation center and ask for a wildlife rehabilitator to visit your school or sponsor a trip to a zoo or wild animal park. For a list of available educational materials contact World Wildlife Fund, 1250 24th Street, NW, Washington, DC 20037, 1-(202) 293-4800.

PURPOSE
This lesson focuses on the crucial role trees play in the environment. Students take a census of nearby trees and use a formula to estimate how much carbon dioxide the trees remove from the air.

BACKGROUND
Trees provide cooling shade in the heat of summer, habitats for animals, and root systems that hold precious soil. They take in carbon dioxide and release oxygen during photosynthesis, countering the effects of the buildup of the greenhouse gas carbon dioxide.

MATERIALS AND METHODS
Before students begin, survey the local area to look for appropriate census sites—the immediate schoolyard, a residential block, or a nearby park. Students will need tape measures and graph paper. Provide regional tree keys to help students identify trees. You may also have to contact maintenance personnel to find out the approximate ages of trees.

TEACHING STRATEGIES
Possible subjects to correlate with this lesson include classification of plants, photosynthesis, transport in plants, exchange of gases in living things, biotic and abiotic factors in the environment, biomes of the world, and pollution of the environment.

POSSIBLE OUTCOMES
Just Do It: The number of trees that students count and map in their census area will vary widely as will their calculations of the potential amount of carbon dioxide absorbed by each tree annually. Although their figures will vary significantly, students will get the idea that planting trees is beneficial, but the trees need to mature before they use a significant amount of carbon dioxide.

Decision Making: 1. Trees help to counter the greenhouse effect by using carbon dioxide during photosynthesis. Students will probably answer that more trees should be planted, but it will take several years for the trees to make a significant change in the amount of carbon dioxide consumed. **2.** Other benefits of having trees include the production of shade, providing habitats for animals, preventing soil erosion, and providing aesthetic beauty. **3.** Planting trees in the southeastern and southwestern corners of a house have the greatest effect on keeping the house cool. **4.** In some areas, recycled cut trees are placed along the shoreline to prevent beach erosion or in wooded trails to prevent flooding.

EXTENSIONS
Contact your state forest and wildlife service or department of natural resources to find out if free seedlings are available to your school district. Call early in the year as many of the seedlings are distributed well before Arbor Day (last Friday in April). For more information about the nationwide campaign to get more trees planted sponsored by American Forestry Association contact Global ReLeaf, PO Box 2000, Washington, DC 20013.

THE RAIN FOREST   ACTIVITY 17

PURPOSE
This lesson focuses on the global impact of rain forest destruction. Students visit stores, take a survey of the products that come from the rain forest, and classify these products into two groups, those that aid the preservation of the rain forest and those that add to its destruction.

BACKGROUND
The rain forest covers only 6 percent of Earth's surface, but it is home to well over half of all species on the planet. As the biodiversity of the rain forests diminishes, species that could be potential sources of new foods or drugs are lost forever.

READINGS
Save the Earth by Jonathan Porritt (Turner Publishing, 1991) contains sections on pollution, global warming, and other topics. Another in-depth look at biodiversity is *Portraits of the Rainforest*, by Adrian Forsyth with photographs by Michael and Patricia Fogden (Camden House, Ontario, Canada, 1990).

MATERIALS AND METHODS
Before students begin the activity, make your own survey of appropriate stores in your community including gift shops, department stores, clothing stores, home furnishing outlets, furniture stores, gourmet food shops, florists, and pet shops. If there are few stores near you, have students look through mail-order catalogues for ideas.

TEACHING STRATEGIES
Possible subjects to correlate with this lesson include the process of evolution, classification of plants and animals, biodiversity, adaptations of organisms to their environment, world biomes, biotic and abiotic factors in the environment, deforestation, and conservation of resources.

POSSIBLE OUTCOMES
Just Do It: Answers will vary but students may find products that support the rain forest include a number of fairly new food items (especially ones containing nuts) and personal care products containing plant oils from the rain forest.

Decision Making: 1. In this question, students are faced with the dilemma of many business people—selling what is environmentally correct or trying to make a profit. Students may wish to debate this important issue. **2.** This question raises the issue of domain of local authorities and has led to many confrontations and even violence. Foreign researches are often at risk when it comes to local development of the economy and inventive diplomacy is needed. **3.** As the rain forests are diminished, more carbon dioxide from human activity is in the atmosphere.

EXTENSIONS
For more information about the rain forest contact Rainforest Alliance, 65 Bleeker Street, New York, NY 10012, 1-(212) 677-1900. Their high school Resource Kit containing a bibliography, poster, and other learning aids is available for $7. For free fact sheets and other educational materials contact the Rainforest Action Network, 450 Sansome, Suite 700, San Francisco, CA 94111, 1-(415) 398-4404.

WHY ARE WETLANDS IMPORTANT?   ACTIVITY 18

PURPOSE
This lesson focuses on wetland habitats. Students observe the effects of nutrients on the growth of wetland organisms and survey some of the organisms that live in this unique habitat.

BACKGROUND
Wetlands are transitional areas between land and a deepwater habitat and include estuaries, swamps, bogs, and areas near lakes, rivers, and streams. Wetlands are among the most productive of all environments and serve as a buffer for neighboring ecosystems. They are characterized by periodic algae and bacteria blooms, natural phenomena that are often stimulated by runoff containing chemicals produced by human activity.

MATERIALS AND METHODS
To set up Part I, students will need algae such as *Spirogyra* from a pond or from a stock culture available from a biological supply house or aquarium supplier,

paper towels, pan balances, beakers, pond water, and three different detergents, at least one of which contains phosphates.

TEACHING STRATEGIES

Possible subjects to correlate with this lesson include life cycles of algae and bacteria, reproduction in aquatic plants and animals, water transport in plants and animals, biotic and abiotic factors in aquatic biomes, and pollution in the environment.

POSSIBLE OUTCOMES

Just Do It: After students have left the beakers in the sunlight for a short time, they are likely to see bubbles of oxygen gas released during photosynthesis. Depending on conditions, students are likely to observe a greater increase in algal mass in the beaker with

phosphate detergent. For Part II: Students should be able to identify the types of wetland found in their region and some of the typical species including endangered species. If students visit a site, they can identify a bloom by the green growth covering the surface of the water.

Decision Making: Students will probably suggest that they would want to know which species would be threatened if there is development. They might suggest also that draining the wetland, which serves to protect the neighboring ecosystems by preventing flooding and absorbing water pollutants, could have a negative impact.

EXTENSIONS

Contact your regional conservation department to find out more about wetlands programs in your area.

BALANCING ACT   ACTIVITY 19

PURPOSE

This lesson focuses on ecological balance. Students conduct and present an in-depth survey of a local environmental site.

BACKGROUND

Every ecosystem has its own unique balance of abiotic and biotic factors. Each habitat has its producers, herbivores, and carnivores that form a pyramid of energy. Scientists study an ecosystem by identifying and quantifying its biotic and abiotic factors.

MATERIALS AND METHODS

Just Do It: For Part I: Scout out possible environmental sites beforehand. Students will need a meter stick or tape measure, mallets, stakes, and string; they will also need dichotomous keys or guide books to determine dominant plant and animal species. For Part II, students will need almanacs for weather information, thermometers or other weather-measuring equipment, and pH paper. For Part III it would be helpful, but not necessary, to use a camera.

TEACHING STRATEGIES

Possible subjects to correlate with this lesson include interaction among the organisms in the environment, biotic and abiotic factors in the environment, biomes of

the world, biological succession, pyramids of energy and biomes within the biolgoical community.

POSSIBLE OUTCOMES

Just Do It: Students should be able to determine some of the dominant plant and animal species of their ecological site, show a typical food chain, and determine abiotic factors such as temperature, rainfall, water and soil conditions. They may display their other results with graphs, and should be able to write a cohesive description of the site.

Decision Making: **1.** Encourage students to answer this question by effectively using their data. **2.** To help students answer this question, go to your local library or planning board for an environmental impact statement (EIS) to which students can compare their answers. **3.** Start a file of articles and letters to the editor that people have written about any parcel of land in your community currently under dispute.

EXTENSIONS

Invite a local official, newspaper editor, environmental activist, developer or a combination of these to come to your class and discuss any local issue of interest to the community.

BE AN EARTHWISE CONSUMER   ACTIVITY 20

PURPOSE

This lesson focuses on the movement toward buying environmentally sound products. Students write a typical shopping list, classify the products by category, then go to a store to find which specific brands of each product are the least harmful to the environment.

BACKGROUND

Every day Americans buy millions of dollars worth of

consumer products, many of which directly or indirectly cause pollution. One way to halt further air and water pollution and help clean up the environment is by buying and using products that contain fewer chemicals and require fewer nonrenewable resources for their production, and use less packaging materials. This trend toward more environmentally-sound products is sometimes called *buying green.*

READINGS

The Green Pages, Your Everyday Shopping Guide to Environmentally Safe Products (The Bennett Information Group, Random House, NY, 1990) has a complete listing of the brand names of green products and a consumer guide organized by laundry, kitchen, nursery, bathroom, yard, and garage.

MATERIALS AND METHODS

Help students get started with their shopping lists the first day of the activity and approve the lists.

TEACHING STRATEGIES

Possible subjects to correlate with this lesson include abiotic and biotic factors in the environment, the process of decomposition, conservation of resources, and pollution in the environment.

POSSIBLE OUTCOMES

Just Do It: Results will vary widely. Ask students to share what they have learned.

Decision Making: 1. Student results will vary. **2.** Students may suggest asking store management to carry the less polluting alternative products. **3.** Ask students to bring in the wrappers of the snack foods they compared and give an oral report of their comparison.

EXTENSIONS

Students may wish to try these two other alternative cleaning agents: for an all-purpose cleaner, mix 5 grams of borax and 6 milliliters of liquid soap in a liter spray bottle of water; to make disinfectant, use 30 grams of borax dissolved in 2 liters of hot water.

WATER, WATER EVERYWHERE?

THE BIG PICTURE

"Water, water everywhere,
Nor any drop to drink."
The Rime of the Ancient Mariner,
Samuel Taylor Coleridge (1772–1834)

In an old poem, a sailor laments that there is sea water all around him, but none of it is fresh water with which to wet his parched lips. At the close of the twentieth century, these lines from the poem take on new meaning. Is there enough clean, fresh water to serve an ever-growing global population?

The Water Cycle   When you turn on the faucet for a glass of water, you are tapping into Earth's water cycle. Water evaporates over bodies of water—the ocean, lakes, and rivers—becomes water vapor, and forms clouds. Within the clouds, water vapor condenses and coalesces into water droplets that fall as precipitation over land and sea. As the rain or snow hits the ground, some is absorbed and some runs off into streams. Streams form rivers and the rivers eventually run downhill toward lakes or oceans. Then the processes of evaporation, condensation, and precipitation repeat themselves. This is called the *water cycle*, a cycle that has recurred for millions of years.

Freshwater Sources   Throughout the world, people draw water from freshwater sources such as streams, rivers, lakes, and groundwater, water held in porous layers of sand or gravel below Earth's surface. Groundwater provides about half of the water used by people in the United States, even those who live in some cities. Everyone expects to turn on a water faucet and see sparkling, pure water, regardless of its source. Water purity is an expectation that is not always met, however. To know something about the water that enters your body each day and is assimilated into your cells, you may want to learn more about where it comes from.

JUST DO IT

1. Research the source of your local water supply. First find out if your water comes from a municipal water supply (your city or town), a private water company, a private well, or some other source.
    a. If your water comes from a well, find out how deep the well is and learn about the structure of rock layers that surround it. You may also make a cross-sectional diagram of the water table or aquifer from which the water is drawn. Compare your source to that of other students in your class.
    b. If you live in a town or city, your water supply may be held in a reservoir. Find out where the original source of the water is and what kind of treatment your water receives. If everyone in your class has the same water source, share the responsibility of contacting your water supplier by sending a clearly-stated letter identifying your class and purpose. Your water supplier may send you a published pamphlet on how water comes to your city.
2. Make a flow chart to show how water gets from its source to the faucet in your home.
3. A watershed is an area drained by different rivers or river systems. Draw a map of your geographical region including mountains and rivers. This will help you determine the area of your watershed.

4. Investigate the method of water purification used in your community. Is the water filtered or chlorinated, or both? Is fluoride added to the water or was it added in the past?
5. Find out how much water your community uses per household per year.
6. Make a list of all of the ways in which you use water in one day. Then estimate how many gallons you use in one year, using this checklist:

WATER USAGE	
Activity	**Approximate volume**
Dishwashing	10 gallons
Toilet	3 gallons
Shower	25 gallons
Bath	35 gallons
Clothes washing	25 gallons
Washing hands/face	0.25 gallons

DECISION MAKING

1. A significant source of water pollution is the solid and chemical wastes that are produced by industry and then dumped into the nearest body of water. Suppose you are on the planning board of your town, and developers seek to locate a factory near your water supply. What questions would you ask when the board met with the developers? How would you use the answers and the data you have collected to justify a position for or against the location?
2. Suppose your area is experiencing a drought. Make a list of changes that you would make to conserve water. Your water supplier may have a water conservation booklet to help you.
3. In some places around the world, as in Saudi Arabia, sea water is an important water source. Modern desalination plants remove the salt and produce fresh water. Is this process a likely solution to water shortages in your region? What are some other possibilities of future water sources?

GOING FURTHER

1. Since the beginning of recorded human activity, civilizations have sprung up around bodies of water—the sea coast, a river, even an oasis in the desert. Trace the history of the settlement of your area and find out if an important waterway or body of water influenced the settlement.
2. Sponsor a water-awareness day in your school. Design posters and find songs or literary themes that have to do with water to incorporate into informative presentations.

SOURCES OF WATER POLLUTION

THE BIG PICTURE

Contaminated Drinking Water Recently hundreds of people became ill in the city of Milwaukee, Wisconsin, and the mayor advised everyone to boil water before using it. The culprit was a microscopic parasite that was living in the water supply and making people sick. Could this happen where you live? In the past, there have been countless other tales of impurities in drinking water, ranging from industrial waste, sewage, and pesticides to fertilizers used in agriculture. According to a report by the U.S. Geological Survey in 1988, every state in the United States has reported some form of contamination of groundwater caused by human activities.

How does this nasty stuff get into drinking water? Water is a solvent—that is, many compounds dissolve in it. Also, the ground is permeable. It acts like a sponge, soaking up pollutants that seep down from above.

Pollutants can spread through permeable rock layers and into groundwater. Water that neither soaks into the ground nor evaporates, but instead flows across Earth's surface and eventually into bodies of water is called *runoff*. Runoff can carry pollutants, especially crop fertilizers and chemicals, into the water supply.

MAJOR WATER POLLUTANTS

- organic solvents such as chemical cleaners and oils used in industry
- gasoline and other petroleum products from leaky tanks and spills
- pesticides, herbicides, and fungicides used to eliminate garden pests and kill weeds and fungi
- road salt used to de-ice roadways
- fertilizers used to grow crops
- septic tanks containing household waste
- garbage dumps without protective linings
- lead from plumbing pipes

JUST DO IT

1. Find out about potential sources of water pollution that may affect your water supply directly. Are there any industries that discharge solid or chemical wastes into nearby waterways? Is your area agricultural? Farmland can be the source of runoff of pesticides and fertilizers. An old garbage dump, even if not in use, can still pollute water as materials leach through the soil into groundwater. Other sources of information about local water pollution may be your local board of health, planning board, or fire department.

2. Make a diagram that shows how possible pollutants may be getting into your water supply.

3. The Environmental Protection Agency (EPA) has identified more than one thousand sources of contamination in drinking water. (There may be at least another thousand not recognized by that agency.) Public water companies must test for at least thirty of these pollutants on a regular basis and monitor over thirty more. Contact the local water supplier and ask for the most recent analysis of compounds and chemicals found in your water. They are required to provide you with the amounts of each of these chemicals found in your water to show that these amounts comply with the EPA standards.

PRIMARY DRINKING WATER CONTAMINANTS (partial list)
- *Microbiological*
   coliform bacteria from human and animal waste
- *Inorganic chemicals (naturally-occurring and often mined substances which are toxic in some way to humans)*

arsenic	cadmium	lead	nitrate	silver
barium	chromium	mercury	selenium	fluoride

- *Organic chemicals which pose health risks, including cancer*

pesticides:	*fuel:*	*solvents:*	*pipe manufacturing:*
endrin	benzene	carbon tetrachloride	vinyl chloride
lindane		trichloroethane	
methoxychlor			
toxaphene			
p-dichlorobenzene			

DECISION MAKING

1. Pollution can come from industrial, residential, or recreational sources. Are there any of these sources of pollution in your area that affect your water supply? What can you do to raise public awareness about this issue?
2. Should you filter the water that comes into your home? Some methods of home treatment include carbon filters, reverse osmosis, distillation, chlorination, and water softeners. Find out more about how these methods work and what contaminants they eliminate.
3. The sales of bottled water in this country have skyrocketed over the last decade. Should you be drinking bottled water? Check the labels on water bottles at the supermarket. Bring in some different kinds of bottled water and have a taste test. Be advised that bottled water has less regulation than the public water supply and may even come from tap water someplace else. Although the label on a bottle of water may state that the water is purified, distilled, or is club soda, the water may still be tap water. Only spring water must actually come from a spring. (New regulations have yet to go into effect for labeling bottled water.)
4. Suppose you live in an area where people value having a beautiful green lawn. In areas of periodic drought, lawns require a great deal of water. In other parts of the country with sufficient rainfall, some people use abundant amounts of chemical fertilizers and pesticides to kill real or imagined pests, such as grubs and crabgrass. These chemicals seep into the groundwater. Discuss alternatives.

GOING FURTHER

Find out how water pollution has affected the recreational use of waterways in your area. How has recreational use been the cause of water pollution?

THE AIR WE BREATHE

THE BIG PICTURE

> *We must now extend the right to breathe*
> *free to every nation and every individual,*
> *for the right to breathe free is the most*
> *basic human right of all.*
> —Reverend Jesse Jackson, Jr.

Is Fresh Air Really Fresh?   Take a deep breath. Whether you are inside a city apartment or outside in the fresh air, your body requires oxygen to function. Oxygen makes up only one-fifth of the gas you breathe in with each inhalation; you may be getting a lot more than what you bargained for. City dwellers get used to traffic-congested highways with vehicles spewing out air pollutants that form a yellow-brown haze. But even if you are off in the pristine wilderness, global wind patterns can be carrying air pollutants to wherever you are.

Staying indoors can be even worse. Inside the home, the air can be contaminated by radon, formaldehyde, or other chemicals. In offices, many people report breathing difficulties, dizziness, and headache, sometimes attributed to poor ventilation systems. This phenomenon has become so common it is known as the *sick building syndrome*.

Steps have been taken to improve the air quality of our environment. The 1990 Clean Air Act, for example, is aimed at further reducing air pollution, with tough standards for the emission of pollutants by motor vehicles and industry smokestacks.

JUST DO IT

Use the list of common air pollutants below to see how the air quality where you live checks out. First, make a large chart with these headings for all your data.

Pollutant	Method of detection	Check It Out	Possible sources

Make a check in the appropriate column if you find evidence of that pollutant in your environment. Also, identify the method of detection. For example, sometimes you can see smog in the air or smell certain chemicals. Sometimes you may use a testing kit, monitoring device, or rely on a news report. If the number of checks is 8 to 10, the air quality in your environment is poor.

COMMON AIR POLLUTANTS

Outdoors
Smog   Refer to newspapers and TV reports for a week. Is there any mention of a smog alert where you live?

Particulates   Do a simple test for particulate pollution (visible particles of soot and ash from burning) by placing some petroleum jelly in a dish and leaving it out on a window sill. Look at the dish every day for a week.

Indoors at home or school
Carbon monoxide   Get a home carbon monoxide detection kit, available at some local hardware stores. Place it in the kitchen, a room near an attached garage, or in your classroom. If your home has an unvented gas stove that uses a continually burning pilot light, it may be giving off carbon monoxide, carbon dioxide, and nitrogen dioxide.

Cigarette smoke   Does anyone you live with smoke in your home? Cigarette smoke is made up of 3000 different chemicals which can cause a variety of ailments. Second-hand smoke is now linked with severe respiratory diseases.

Radon   Find out if radon gas is naturally present in the soil or bedrock in your area. Home test kits are available for radon detection. Radon emits alpha particles, radioactive emissions that may cause cancer over a long period of time. Find out whether a radon test has been made at your school. Use two checks if both your home and school have a radon problem.

Asbestos   Asbestos, a natural building material that is fireproof, was used in outdoor shingles and as pipe insulation. However, old asbestos can shed tiny particles that become airborne. When inhaled and trapped in the lungs, the particles may cause cancer or emphysema (an inflammation of the lungs that can be fatal). Many asbestos-abatement programs have been initiated in schools, in order to remove old asbestos. Find out whether this procedure has been necessary in your school.

Formaldehyde   This organic chemical is used in the making of foam found in rugs, furniture, insulation, and wrinkle-resistant bed linens. You can often detect its odor in such products when they are new. If you have in your home any of these items that are under one year old, make a check. (Formaldehyde test kits are also available.)

Ozone   Do you use a copy machine frequently or have hobbies that involve welding? Ozone forms from oxygen in the presence of electricity. Excessive ozone can cause eye and lung irritation.

Community
Sick building syndrome   Have there been any reports of any office buildings in your community in which people have suffered unexplained sickness?

EPA alert   Has the EPA ever visited your area to investigate a problem related to air pollution? If the problem was not identified and corrected, make a check.

DECISION MAKING

1. If you judged the air quality to be poor, what can you do? Whom should you alert?
2. Industries are fined if they do not conform to government emission standards, but sometimes the laws are not enforced. How might you inform a legislator from your area that air pollution laws are not being enforced?
3. Industries that pollute less than they are allowed to under law can sell their leftover pollution allowances to another company. Do you think this is right? Discuss.

GOING FURTHER

1. On any given school day, student parking lots are full although bus transportation is available. What are some sensible nonpolluting alternatives to driving a car?
2. On some roadways, new lanes of traffic are being built to encourage car pooling. Is this a worthwhile idea? Why or why not?

IS IT GETTING HOT IN HERE?

THE BIG PICTURE

Imagine sweltering summer afternoons as temperatures zoom to well over 100°F for days on end. Leaking dikes hold back flood waters that threaten coastal cities. The shapes of familiar shorelines are lost as rising sea levels etch out new ones. These are pictures of the not-too-distant future painted by some scientists, based on data that indicate a rising trend in average global temperatures. According to these scientists, something is turning up Earth's thermostat at an alarming rate, and they speculate that the cause may be the greenhouse effect, increased by human activity.

The Greenhouse Effect   The *greenhouse effect* is a natural process that keeps Earth warm enough to be hospitable to life. Here is how it works. When sunlight strikes Earth's surface, it is absorbed and changed to heat, which warms land and ocean. The heat from the surface is then radiated back toward space as longer wavelengths of infrared energy. Much of this energy is lost in space, but some of these longer wavelengths are absorbed by gases in the atmosphere and redirected toward Earth. Thus, some of the sun's energy becomes trapped as heat in the lower atmosphere and on Earth's surface, much as a greenhouse traps heat on a sunny day. Water vapor in the atmosphere contributes most to the greenhouse effect. Carbon dioxide also contributes significantly; other gases, including methane, ozone, and nitrogen oxides, play a part, too. Without the greenhouse effect our planet would be cold—perhaps over 50 degrees colder than at present. With too great a greenhouse effect, the planet could be an oven, like Venus, with its blanket of carbon dioxide and blazing surface temperatures of hundreds of degrees.

Although CO_2 contributes to the greenhouse effect on Earth much less than does water vapor, the effect of CO_2 has been discussed a great deal in recent years because the CO_2 content of the atmosphere has been increasing since the Industrial Revolution. Other greenhouse gases have also increased. At an observatory in Hawaii, scientists measuring atmospheric CO_2 over the last thirty years have found that CO_2 levels have risen by 25 percent. So, too, the average temperature of Earth has been rising steadily and, within the last several decades, the rise has been sharper. Many new heat records were set in the 1980s. Is the rise in CO_2 related to the rise in temperature? Although a relationship has by no means been established, if there is such a connection, some scientists say, then the extended forecast is for a warming trend. Using data to extrapolate into the future, these scientists predict temperatures could rise from 3°F to 9°F over the next century. If this rise occurs, much of the ice in polar regions will melt. The Environmental Protection Agency predicts that sea levels could rise from 5 to 15 inches, with periodic heat waves and droughts more common.

The cause of this warming trend is believed by some to be an increased greenhouse effect due to increased CO_2 produced during the process of fuel combustion. The gas methane is even better at trapping heat than CO_2. Methane comes from natural gas but is also released in mining and refining processes and is a by-product of the decay of organic materials. CFCs (chlorofluorocarbons) can also contribute to the greenhouse effect, because they trap heat 10 000 to 20 000 times more efficiently than CO_2.

For the following activity, assume that the increase in greenhouse effect is attributable to increased greenhouse gases.

JUST DO IT

1. Make a pie chart to show the information below.

   Percentages of global warming attributable to greenhouse gases
Carbon dioxide	49%
Methane	18%
CFCs	14%
Nitrous oxide	6%
Other	13%

2. Using the statistics below, make a line graph to show the increase of carbon dioxide in the atmosphere over the last 130 years. (Figures are approximate).

Year	1860	1880	1900	1920	1940	1960	1980	1990
CO_2 content of air in parts per million (ppm)	290	292	296	302	309	320	335	350

   a. Calculate the average annual increase in CO_2 for the period 1860 to 1880.

   b. Compare that increase to the average annual increase in CO_2 content in the decade 1980 to 1990.

   c. Since 1988, the average annual increase has jumped to 2 ppm per year. Using this information, determine what the CO_2 content would be in the year 2000.

3. Follow the weather report for two weeks and compare your data with the average temperature in your region for this time of year. Then write a scenario of what it would be like if the average temperature of your region increased by 7°F.

DECISION MAKING

1. People in the United States produce more CO_2 as a result of human activity than people in any other country. How would this affect how you might represent your country at a conference on global warming?

2. Trees use CO_2 and produce oxygen during photosynthesis. Suppose you headed a committee that proposed that trees should be planted along a heavily traveled highway. What kind of proposal would you write? What ideas would you include?

GOING FURTHER

Burning 1 gallon of gas produces almost 20 pounds of CO_2. The typical American car burns over 800 gallons of gas a year. In one year, one car can emit 800 × 20 or 16 000 pounds of CO_2. How many miles are driven on those 800 gallons depends on the car's fuel efficiency—the number of miles it gets to the gallon (MPG). Use the following data to make a pictograph to help persuade someone to drive a fuel-efficient car.

Car model	MPG	Tons of CO_2 emitted over car's life
X	45.0	25.93
Y	27.5	37.71
Z	18.0	57.75

SAVE OUR SKINS: OZONE DEPLETION AND SKIN DISORDERS

THE BIG PICTURE

If the atmosphere is Earth's blanket of air, then the ozone layer is Earth's security blanket. But where this blanket appears to have worn thin, the problem is more than one of cold feet.

The Weakening Ozone Layer Far above Earth's surface, in the stratosphere, high-energy waves of ultraviolet light from the sun bombard oxygen atoms, which usually travel in pairs, and split them. The freed oxygen atoms then team up with oxygen pairs to form molecules containing three oxygen atoms. These O_3 molecules are known as *ozone*. Ozone formation blocks some of the UV radiation from reaching Earth's surface. But in the 1970s scientists detected a weakening in the ozone layer. By the mid-1980s they began to document the progress of the thinning of this important shield.

What is causing the weakening of the ozone shield is the migration of compounds released on Earth's surface upwards to the ozone layer, where they split millions of ozone molecules. The prime offenders are a group of compounds called CFCs, or chlorofluorocarbons. These compounds are used as coolants in refrigerators and air conditioners, propellants in spray cans, in the manufacture of plastic foam, and as solvents for cleaning computer chips. While stable near Earth's surface, CFCs break up in the upper atmosphere and the chlorine atoms released react with ozone, changing it to ordinary oxygen that does not absorb UV radiation. A single chlorine atom can be involved in many such reactions, destroying as many as 10 000 ozone molecules. Other compounds called *halons* contain bromine, an element with chemical properties similar to those of chlorine. For this reason the halons, commonly used in fire extinguishers, also endanger the ozone.

The Danger of UV Radiation Too much UV radiation (especially the band of wave lengths known as UVB) on living tissue is harmful to DNA and can weaken the immune system in both humans and animals. UV radiation is also what "tans" human skin tissue in some instances but can also cause skin cancer—melanoma—which may not show up for many years. Dermatologists report that for every 1 percent decrease in the ozone layer there is a 2 percent increase in the incidence of skin cancer. UVB also damages the delicate tissues of the eye, causing cataracts. The thinning ozone may also be affecting countless organisms from crops and cattle in the fields to the plankton and whales of the oceans. To counter these effects, there has been a worldwide effort to phase out CFCs. However, many of these compounds are still in the atmosphere. People must protect themselves from dangerous levels of UVB by wearing headgear and sunglasses and by applying effective sunblocks to their skin.

JUST DO IT

1. Scientists have been measuring the size of the ozone hole that forms annually over Antarctica every September. Because it is the beginning of spring in the Southern Hemisphere, the ultraviolet light shines down into the ocean waters, affecting the reproduction of algae and thus the entire food chain.

a. You will need a piece of graph paper (preferably with small squares) to chart the increase in the size of the ozone hole. First look at the pictures shown.

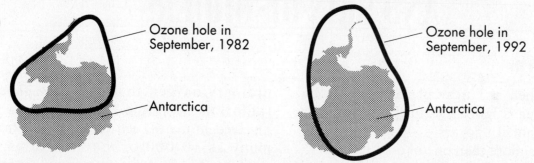

Ozone hole in September, 1982

Antarctica

Ozone hole in September, 1992

Antarctica

b. Trace the pictures onto graph paper. Count the number of squares each ozone hole is covering. How has the hole grown from 1982 to 1992? Express your answer as a percent.

2. Use a map or globe to determine your latitude. Use your newspaper's weather page or listen to the weather report to find out how many hours of daylight you had today. What time of year is it? Should you be wearing a sunblock?

3. Go to a drug store and take a survey of the sunblock and other sun products that are offered for sale. What does SPF mean? Count how many different products have an SPF equal to or greater than 15. How many products are available that offer no UV protection?

4. Look at the selection of sunglasses. Calculate what percentage of the sunglasses available offer protection against UVB. Does UVB protection cost more?

DECISION MAKING

1. Among the people you know, is it still socially acceptable behavior to lie in the sun unprotected to get a tan? How can you work to change this? Would you tell a friend if you thought he or she should be applying sunblock? What would you tell a group of students about the long-term risks of exposure to UV light?

2. Suppose you need to buy a fire extinguisher for your home. Would you be willing to pay more for one that does not contain halons? Explain.

3. Make inquiries at your local auto repair shops and appliance stores. Ask how the shops deal with broken air conditioners and refrigerators. Find out if these shops recycle the coolants or just release them into the atmosphere. What can you do to inform shop owners that they are causing a problem?

4. Suppose you visit a foreign country and find that the only hairspray that you can buy is an aerosol with CFC propellant. Would you buy a can of hairspray or not?

GOING FURTHER

Set up a mock international conference on the ozone layer. Different students can represent different countries, some of which have supported a ban or gradual phaseout of compounds that harm the ozone layer and others that continue to use these compounds. Support your government's views with diagrams, charts, and logical arguments.

TOXIC WASTE—WHERE DOES IT GO?

THE BIG PICTURE

Teach your children what we have taught our children, that the Earth is our mother. Whatever befalls the Earth befalls the sons of the Earth. Man did not weave the web of life. He is merely a strand in it. Whatever he does to the web, he does to himself.

—Chief Seattle of the Suquamish tribe
to President Franklin Pierce, 1854

The people of Love Canal, near Buffalo, New York, did not know what would befall them when they moved into a new housing development built on top of a canal filled with toxic wastes. Soon residents noticed foul-smelling ooze seeping into their basements. Officials found cancer-causing PCB chemicals, and by 1978 hundreds of residents were evacuated. But it was already too late for those people who suffered from epilepsy, liver disease, nervous disorders, and many birth defects as a result of contamination.

Sources of Toxic Waste There are about 250 million tons of toxins produced every year in this country, enough for every individual to have a personal pile of toxins equal to the weight of a car. Toxic wastes are derived mainly from the making, use, and disposal of chemicals. There are thousands of chemicals in use today, many of them carcinogenic—cancer-causing—if people or animals are exposed to them. Even chemicals no longer in use can persist in human body tissue for an entire lifetime. Many chemicals are fat-soluble rather than water-soluble, and once ingested, the chemicals are stored within the body.

In some places people have begun to organize to get toxic waste out of residential areas. In New York City, for example, an environmental action group consisting of many teenagers who call themselves the *Toxic Avengers* has formed to educate the citizens and work with lawyers to rid their neighborhood of a facility that stores radioactive and explosive wastes. But although industries produce toxic wastes, consumers—ordinary people—continue to use many of the products made with toxic substances. Many household cleaners, bug sprays, and even art supplies can contain toxins. When these products are disposed of, they may wind up in a landfill, turning it into a toxic dump. When the products are used at home and flushed away down the drain, the toxins go into septic systems and possibly into the water supply or the food chain. Do you think there are any hidden toxins in your home?

JUST DO IT

1. Take a survey of the toxins that you have right at home by comparing what you find to the household hazardous wastes checklist below. If you discover a product that is not included, add it to the list.
2. Draw up a floor plan of your home, showing each room and any outside areas you use. Then for each room, list any of these toxins that you have found there.

Living area

ammonia-based cleaners	oven cleaner	clothes that are dry
room deodorizers (air fresheners)	spot remover	cleaned (dry cleaning
furniture polish	moth balls	fluids such as
laundry detergents with phosphates or bleach	drain cleaner	perchlorethylene are toxic)

Hobby area
old paint
paint thinner
brush cleaner
paint remover
wood preservative
photography supplies
art supplies (paints,
  solvent-based markers)

Garage
antifreeze
motor oil
rust preservatives
diesel fuel

Yard
insect spray
weed or poison
  ivy killer
swimming pool
  chemicals

DECISION MAKING

1. Now that you know some of the toxins that you live with everyday, can you think of some alternatives that are nonpolluting? Explain the advantages and disadvantages of these alternatives.

2. Environmental activists propose that if consumers stop buying and using products that contain toxins, manufacturers will stop making them. What do you think? Give reasons for your views.

3. There may be as many as 300 000 hazardous waste sites in the United States. The Environmental Protection Agency (EPA) established a Superfund in 1980 that provides money to clean up the worst toxic waste sites. Work so far on the sites has been painfully slow. Find out if there are any dumps in your area slated for Superfund cleanup. What progress has been made? What are the problems?

4. The amount of used motor oil thrown out each year in the United States is greater than the 11 million gallons of the 1989 Alaskan oil spill. Visit several car repair shops and gasoline stations. Find out what they do with their used oil. Find out where you can bring used motor oil for disposal in your community and prepare a list of such places others can use. How can you convince friends who work on their cars to recycle their oil?

GOING FURTHER

1. Since the mid-1980s, a right-to-know law was passed that requires local companies to tell people in a community exactly what kinds of toxins are being produced. This means that you have the right to ask companies for such a list and to find out what they do with their toxic waste. Is there a company nearby that produces toxins? If so, write a polite letter of inquiry and find out what chemical wastes are produced and how they dispose of them. Share your information in a class discussion.

2. Suppose a chemical company in your area has been given a ten-year extension to remove the toxic mess they have created. Do you think this is right? Why or why not? Why do you think the extension was given? What could you do to speed up the process?

ORGANICALLY GROWN

THE BIG PICTURE

Organic foods are foods produced under a system of ecological soil management that relies on building humus levels through crop rotation, recycling organic wastes, applying balanced mineral amendments, and using varieties resistant to disease and pests.
— The Organic Foods Production Association

Have you ever eaten an organic apple? It may not have been as red, as big, or as perfect in appearance as another apple you might buy at the supermarket, but it does have an important advantage. It has been grown without the use of chemical insecticides or fertilizers.

The Threat of Pesticides   On large commercial farms, insects, rodents, and weeds multiply quickly because of favorable living conditions and concentrated food supplies. Farmers have responded to problems of pests by spraying with enormous quantities of insecticides, rodenticides, and herbicides. But the sad part is that only a tiny percentage of all insecticides actually reach a pest on a plant. Likewise, of all the tons of fertilizer applied to the soil, only a fraction can be absorbed and used by plants. The remainder drifts down into the soil, where it is washed away as runoff that pollutes the land and water. Because pesticides can be ingested by people and animals, they pose a threat to human health. The pesticide DDT, banned over twenty years ago, continues to be found in human tissue and is a likely cause of cancer.

Integrated Pest Management   Some farmers have another approach to the pest problem, called Integrated Pest Management, or IPM. As its name implies, IPM uses a variety of pest controls, most of them natural. Sometimes the pests are kept from the plant by screens or other mechanical means. Certain oils may be applied to plant parts to interfere with some stage of an insect's life cycle. Sometimes a natural predator is found that preys on the specific insect that attacks a specific plant. When added to a field or garden, the predator consumes hundreds of insect pests. Occasionally farmers that employ IPM do use small amounts of pesticides, but with great reservation.

A certified organic farmer may employ some of the natural pest controls suggested by IPM, but never uses any sprayed pesticides. And, instead of using chemical fertilizers such as concentrated nitrates and phosphates, organic farmers build up the soil by rotating crops and using natural fertilizer, such as recycled organic wastes. On a smaller scale, home gardeners can apply organic farming techniques by using compost for fertilizer. Compost is made from organic plant matter that has been broken down by bacteria into rich, dark humus soil.

JUST DO IT

Does your school have a garden or greenhouse that is used for science experiments? Perhaps the addition of a compost pile will turn that site into an organic garden. There are many variations in making compost. Here is a recipe for "quick" compost.

1. Pick a level, well-drained spot in full sun.
2. To build a bin to hold the compost, decide which kinds of materials are available to you at little or no cost. You can use scrap lumber, chicken wire, or even cinder blocks.
3. Use enough building material to make a four-sided box having dimensions of at least 1 meter by 1 meter by 1 meter.

4. Cover the bottom with a layer of coarse organic material, such as twigs, hay, or wood chips. The idea is to allow for air circulation from beneath the pile.

5. Sprinkle the layer with a little water.

6. Cover the coarse layer with a mixture of soil, grass, and garden clippings. Add kitchen waste, such as fruit and vegetable peelings, egg shells, even coffee grounds, but use no greasy animal products.

7. Alternate these layers several times and sprinkle with water until your compost pile reaches a height of at least 1 meter.

8. You may cover the pile with black plastic. What purpose might the plastic serve?

9. Periodically turn the pile with a shovel. The center will be the "hot spot" of decomposition.

10. In as little as four weeks, you may be able to use the compost in the pile to feed house plants and garden plants, shrubs, and trees.

DECISION MAKING

1. If your compost is used in a garden, what do you think the effects will be? Could you convince others in your community to build compost bins in their yards? Some city-dwellers have had success with composting in barrels inside their apartments to use in window gardens.

2. Buy some produce at a health food store or organic farm. Compare a real organic apple with a shiny, waxed commercially-grown apple from a supermarket. Sketch both apples. Notice the differences in shape, texture, and size. Do a taste test. Which tastes better? What are the advantages and disadvantages of each?

3. Alar, a trade name for the chemical daminozide, is a plant growth regulator that makes apples redden more deeply and ripen more slowly. Alar was approved for use in 1963 before strict laws about product testing were enforced; however, in 1989, Alar was found to be a cancer-causing agent in some test animals. When word of this became public, many people were alarmed. Mothers especially had great concern for the health of their children. Alar was eventually withdrawn from the American market. Although the government now sets stricter standards for chemical residues found in fruits and vegetables, the standards still may not really be appropriate for children. Can you think of some reasons why? What might be done in such cases?

4. Some communities have convinced authorities that it would be better not to spray weed killer in public parks. Would you rather tolerate dandelions or smell potentially dangerous chemical herbicides in your favorite park? Do you think similar restrictions are appropriate for private lawns?

GOING FURTHER

1. Visit an organic farm and inquire about how farmers deal with insect pests and what they use for fertilizer. Summarize your findings and share them in a class discussion.

2. Find out if there is an agricultural agency in your area. Ask an expert if IPM is used to curb insect populations in commercial farms near you. Prepare diagrams to show what food chain makes this technique effective.

HOLD ON TO THAT SOIL

THE BIG PICTURE

I will run a furrow with my plough,
I will press my spade through the sod
and turn it up underneath . . .
Behold this compost! Behold it well!
—Walt Whitman, "This Compost,"
from *Leaves of Grass*, 1856

The Importance of Soil   Sod, soil, dirt, mud, compost, land, sacred ground, clods of earth—whether common or poetic, these words are all names for something that we take for granted everyday, the ground beneath our feet. Though much of the soil around you may be covered by buildings or pavement, your life still depends on the healthy soil used for growing the food you eat. Dark humus soil, rich in organic material, provides essential nutrients absorbed by growing plants. When you eat plants, whether munching on an apple or crunching on corn chips, those very same nutrients absorbed by the plant will be absorbed by your cells and become part of your body.

Soil Depletion   Large-scale farming practices have led to a depletion of this precious resource, soil. In the corn-belt state of Iowa, with some of the richest soil in the United States, tons of fertile topsoil are washed away by erosion each year. The practice of intensive farming of the same crops year after year depletes the soil of nutrients. The persistent use of chemical fertilizers also harms the soil. Because fertilizers make essential elements like nitrogen immediately available to plants, the plant roots do not spread out and loosen soil very much, leading to soil compaction. Although soil-conservation techniques like contour plowing and crop rotation are used, there is still a net loss of good soil. On a smaller scale, you can find evidence of soil depletion and erosion right in your own community.

JUST DO IT

Part I   In this part of the activity you can examine the soil from your school grounds and make a soil profile. The activity can also be conducted with soil from a vacant lot or other nearby area.

1. Take a good look at the soil on your school grounds. With your teacher's permission, dig up a small amount from several different locations and place the samples of soil on white paper towels.
2. Examine the samples with a hand lens. Note the contents, the size and color of the grains. Make a detailed drawing. How do samples from different parts of the school grounds compare? Are they different? If so, why do you think they might be different? If they do not differ, why do you think this is so?
3. Use library resources to find a map of soil types around the country. Identify the general soil type for your area. Try to determine whether your soil samples match this type. Use other reference materials if necessary.
4. Follow your teacher's recommendations about disposing of the soil after you have finished your analysis.
5. Outside your classroom and in your community, look for any road cuts or new construction sites in which different layers of soil are exposed. See if you can distinguish between the topsoil and the layers of subsoil underneath. The layers are known as *horizons*. Topsoil is usually labeled horizon A, and layers of subsoil

below it are named horizon B, horizon C, and so on. Make a detailed drawing or take a photograph of the horizons. This is called a *soil profile*.

Part II   In this part of the activity you will investigate the issue of soil erosion and its prevention.

6. Design a demonstration to show how soil erosion can take place. You may use soil, water, a tray, a fan, or other materials approved by your teacher. Use your set-up to demonstrate soil erosion for your class.

7. Form a *Soil Erosion Patrol*. Look carefully around your school grounds and in your community for locations that are undergoing erosion. Are there unprotected hillsides or beaches nearby that look as if wind or water is carrying off soil? Take photographs or draw pictures of how the site looks before and after a storm.

8. Compare an erosion site to similar areas that are not undergoing erosion. Investigate and explain what is holding the soil and preventing erosion in those areas.

DECISION MAKING

1. What are some of the methods used in your area to reduce erosion? Are retaining walls built? Are certain trees, bushes, or grasses planted to reduce erosion?

2. If you have discovered an environmentally sensitive site nearby in which erosion could be prevented, write a proposal stating what action could alleviate the problem. Then, form an interested group of friends, and try to obtain permission to carry out your proposal.

3. Make a map of your community that indicates agricultural, residential, and commercial areas. Which areas have the most problems with erosion control? Are there any areas in which the soil has been contaminated by toxic waste?

4. Do people in your community create "shortcuts" by walking through fields, woods, or empty lots? Are recreational vehicles commonly driven along unpaved trails in such areas? Do these vehicles make deep ruts in the soil? Discuss how recreational use of the land can cause erosion. Discuss ways in which this erosion can be controlled and why there might be opposition to implementing such plans.

GOING FURTHER

Find out which soil conservation agency or agencies are active in your state or county. Write to the agency and ask if a soil conservationist can visit your school. Inquire about the particular soil problems that are common in your area, and ask the conservationist to test the soil on the school grounds. Compare the results of that soil test with your own observations.

ENERGY: RENEWABLE AND NONRENEWABLE

THE BIG PICTURE

The planet right now needs a place like this!
—Sister Paula Gonzalez, Director of Earth
Connection, describing a solar-heated
house made of recycled materials

Sister Paula Gonzalez thinks that chicken coops are for more than just housing chickens. Using an old chicken coop, scrap materials, and a lot of volunteer help, she built a 1200-square foot, solar-heated house in Cincinnati, Ohio and named it *La Casa del Sol*. "The house of the sun" sounds pretty unlikely in Cincinnati, which is cloudy half the year and has below-average yearly temperatures. Yet, with this innovative approach to solar heating, the house is kept at a very comfortable temperature at a cost of only $30 per month.

Solar energy   Throughout the country, buildings with a *passive solar* design employ windows and special construction materials that absorb the sun's energy and change it to heat to warm the building. Over 50 million American families live in *active solar* homes which use solar collectors, as well as mechanical devices such as pumps or fans, to transfer heat to different parts of the home. Approximately 10 000 American homes are equipped with rooftop modules of *photovoltaic cells*—devices that can convert the sun's energy directly into electricity to be used for lighting and appliances. Whether used for heating or for the generation of electricity, solar energy is considered a renewable energy source, because the sun's radiant energy is continuously striking the planet's surface. Harnessing this energy requires technology, but does not pollute the environment.

Fossil fuels   Do you know where your electric energy comes from? More than likely it is generated at a large power plant that burns fossil fuels such as coal, oil, or natural gas. Fuel is burned to heat water, creating steam that drives enormous turbines. The turbines spin generators, which in turn produce electrical energy. Fuel-burning power plants use up valuable fossil fuels that are irreplaceable and thus are considered nonrenewable sources of energy.

Other sources of energy   Other large power plants in the United States may be hydroelectric, those that use falling water as an energy source, or nuclear, those that harness energy from the breakdown of atoms. These kinds of power plants do not rely on fossil fuels, but they can still cause pollution and may present other hazards. Although some communities utilize hydroelectric or nuclear power, when the majority of people in this country flip a switch, the power usually comes from a nonrenewable source.

In some places, usually on a much smaller scale, energy is generated from a source that is renewable, a source that replenishes itself. These alternative sources include solar, wind, and geothermal power—heat from within Earth. These alternative forms of energy usually do not cause pollution but can be used only where resources make them practical. For example, almost the entire country of Iceland is heated by geothermal energy made available by that island nation's volcanic activity. Geysers throughout the island shoot boiling-hot water from within Earth. This water can be piped into buildings. The Rance River in France, the mouth of which has a strong incoming ocean tide, is the site of a power plant that uses tidal energy. A windy hillside east of San Francisco is dotted with modern windmills that generate electricity. What other alternative energy sources you have seen or read about?

JUST DO IT

Set up and use solar energy devices to prepare a meal and clean up afterward.

1. Plan a lunch menu that can be cooked easily, such as hot dogs, and other foods that require only reheating.
2. Design and test your own solar cooker, using materials such as a foil-lined trough or pan and/or mirrors to direct sunlight. (You may want to refer to some designs in magazines or books at the library.) Be careful not to burn yourself! The temperature at the focus of some solar heaters can be hot enough to weld metal.
3. Design and test a method for making a solar-powered mini-hot-water heater. You will need a suitable container in which the water will be heated when exposed to the sun. Also devise a way to pour out the water, once the temperature has been raised. Experiment with containers made of different materials and of different colors to find a way to raise the temperature of cold water so that it is hot enough to be used for washing dishes and utensils.
4. When your designs are complete, plan for a day on which you can bring in food and prepare lunch, using your solar cooker. Also bring in recyclable plates and napkins and reusable utensils.
5. Use the solar-heated water to wash the lunch dishes.

DECISION MAKING

1. Do you live in a part of the country that receives enough sunlight to use solar power? Do you live in a solar-heated house or would you want to live in one? Why or why not?
2. Do you live in a place where there are windy hillsides suitable for wind-powered generators? Are there any nearby wind-powered generators? What percent of the community's power do they produce? What are some objections to wind-powered generators?
3. Are there other possible alternative energy sources where you live? Do you think the government should spend tax dollars for the exploration and construction of alternative energy plants? Give reasons for your position.

GOING FURTHER

Find a suitable design for a wind-powered generator and build a small model that is based on that design. Investigate how modern technology is being applied to enhance the efficiency of these machines.

WHAT'S YOUR ENERGY QUOTIENT?

THE BIG PICTURE

In 1988, the 3600 people of Osage, Iowa started what turned out to be a very popular energy conservation program. By fixing leaky windows, replacing old furnaces, and insulating hot-water heaters, they managed to save the small town about $1.2 million in energy costs that year.

Electricity Use in the United States How much electricity does your community use? People in the United States use more electricity per person than do people in any other country. Even an industrial factory in the United States uses more electric energy than a similar factory in Europe or Japan. About 75 percent of the national demand for electricity is for buildings—schools, shops, hospitals, apartment buildings, and houses. Of all the power generated in the United States, about one-third is used in homes for heating, cooling, lighting, and appliances.

Using Electric Energy Efficiently The good news is that, since the mid-1970s, improvements in construction technology introduced features such as better insulation, double- and triple-glazed windows, and passive solar heating. These features improved efficiency in heating and cooling and cut energy demands significantly. Energy demands can be further reduced when people use more energy-efficient appliances, such as those made after 1987. In that year, Federal laws mandated improved efficiency for all major household appliances. People can further reduce energy consumption by using the newest lighting technology, which includes more efficient incandescent bulbs and fluorescent lights.

Between 15 percent and 25 percent of home energy costs are for lighting. Do you keep lights on, even during the day? Suppose that you kept a 100-watt incandescent light bulb going 12 hours a day for a year. To keep that bulb lit, the power plant that serves your home might need to burn hundreds of pounds of fuel that would in turn release hundreds of pounds of carbon dioxide into the air. The cost of lighting that one bulb might increase your yearly utility bill by $50.

JUST DO IT

There is an energy-survey form on pages 20 and 21. You can use it to find your energy quotient (*EQ*). Take the energy survey twice—once for your home and once for your school. Be sure to have adult permission and cooperation first. Some questions may apply more to a home than to a school. Award 1 point for every *Yes* answer on the survey. The closer your energy quotient is to 30, the more efficient the building.

TURN THE PAGE TO BEGIN THE SURVEY. →

ENERGY SURVEY

A. Lighting   Yes   No

1. Are there low wattage or fluorescent bulbs in each light fixture
   where possible?   ❏   ❏
2. Are most lights turned off at night or when people are not around? ❏   ❏
3. Are outdoor security lights kept on all night, instead of being activated
   by a motion detector?   ❏   ❏
4. Are light bulbs and fixtures cleaned regularly? Dust can dim the
   lights.   ❏   ❏
5. Are energy-saver or frosted bulbs used where possible?   ❏   ❏

B. Heating the building   Yes   No

6. Do the windows have storm windows or plastic coverings? These
   can reduce heating costs by 15 percent.   ❏   ❏
7. Are all windows and doors free from drafts? As a test, move a
   lighted candle slowly all around each window or door frame.
   If the flame does not flicker, no energy is being lost.
   CAUTION: *Take great care with open flames. Be sure there are no*
   flammable materials, such as curtains or drapes, around windows
   and doors.   ❏   ❏
8. Are the windows double- or triple-glazed where possible?   ❏   ❏
9. Are there insulating drapes over exposed windows?   ❏   ❏
10. Are heaters and radiators periodically cleaned to maintain
    efficiency?   ❏   ❏
11. Is the thermostat set at 68°F or lower?   ❏   ❏
12. Do people in the building dress properly for the season instead of
    relying on indoor heating?   ❏   ❏
13. Is the heating system periodically checked for efficiency?
    Well-adjusted oil or gas burners save heating costs.   ❏   ❏
14. Is the attic or roof insulated?   ❏   ❏
15. Is the building well caulked where the building meets the
    foundation and where plumbing, wires, and vents come
    out of the exterior walls?   ❏   ❏

	Yes	No
C. Heating hot water		

16. Does the hot water heater have a blanket of insulation wrapped around it? Newer models are better insulated than older ones. ❏ ❏

17. Are bathroom showers equipped with devices that restrict water flow? These limit the flow to two gallons per minute and can reduce hot water use by 50 percent. ❏ ❏

18. Are *warm* or *cool* washing machine settings used rather than *hot*? About 90 percent of the energy used by a washing machine goes into heating water. ❏ ❏

19. Is the dishwasher run only when it is full and are energy-saving cycles used when possible? ❏ ❏

	Yes	No
D. Cooling the building		

20. Are area fans used instead of, or along with, air conditioners? ❏ ❏

21. Is the air-conditioning system the right size for the area? ❏ ❏

22. Have efficient air conditioners been purchased? Look at the unit to see if the Seasonal Energy Efficiency Ratio (SEER) is high. ❏ ❏

23. Is the air conditioner well maintained and are filters clean? ❏ ❏

	Yes	No
E. Using appliances		

24. Is the refrigerator defrosted regularly, if it is not frost-free? ❏ ❏

25. Is the back of the refrigerator vacuumed regularly? The condenser coils and air vents need to be cleaned with a vacuum cleaner. This is especially important for older, less energy-efficient models. ❏ ❏

26. Are glass rather than metal pans used in the oven? They conduct heat more evenly and stay warm longer. ❏ ❏

27. Is a microwave oven used when possible? It uses from 70 percent to 80 percent less electricity than a conventional oven does. ❏ ❏

28. Are power tools properly maintained, grounded, and unplugged when not in use? ❏ ❏

29. Do you turn off TVs, radios, computers, video games, stereos, and CD players when you are finished using them? ❏ ❏

30. Do you maintain other electronic equipment so that it runs efficiently and is shut off when not in use? ❏ ❏

Your energy quotient *(EQ)* is the total number of *Yes* answers.

EQ = _____

DECISION MAKING

1. Now that you have seen your *EQ*, were you surprised? To which questions did you answer *No*? What can you do to change those negatives to positives and cut down on energy consumption?
2. Compare your *EQ* to those of other class members. What is the class average? What do you think is an acceptable *EQ*? What are your reasons?
3. Some utility companies offer rebates to people who purchase certain energy-efficient appliances. Some utilities sell or give away energy-saving fluorescent bulbs. Find out if this service is available in your area.
4. Electricity bills are usually calculated in kilowatt-hours. One kilowatt-hour is the amount of energy needed to deliver 1000 watts of power for one hour. Look at the sample electric bills below. Each bill is accompanied by a graph that helps customers understand their electric usage by comparing year-to-year use, as well as providing the average temperature for the billing period. The bill also includes a comparison to average customer use. What happened to energy use in this household from one winter to the next? From one summer to the next? Can you think of reasons for the changes? How does this customer compare to the average customer in energy use for the two seasons? What appliances do you think this household uses in winter and in summer that make energy use differ from the average?

Meter Readings (Summer)

Sep 21	37297 Actual	
Jul 22	35872 Actual	
Use:	61 Days	1425 KWH

Total Cost: $232.22

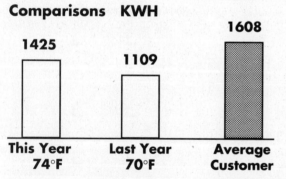

Comparisons KWH

- This Year 74°F — 1425
- Last Year 70°F — 1109
- Average Customer — 1608

Meter Readings (Winter)

Jan 22	30544 Actual	
Nov 20	28001 Actual	
Use:	63 Days	2543 KWH

Total Cost: $368.89

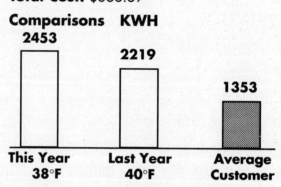

Comparisons KWH

- This Year 38°F — 2453
- Last Year 40°F — 2219
- Average Customer — 1353

GOING FURTHER

1. Take a look at the electric meter in your apartment building or home. Learn how to read it.
2. Find out the name and address of your local utility company. Write them a polite letter and ask for an energy conservation guide, which most utilities publish. Decide if there are enough useful tips. Do you think the company should be doing more to educate consumers about conservation?
3. Try using as little electricity as possible for one day. How did you manage? Did you think the energy saved was worth the inconvenience you experienced?

HOW MANY IS A CROWD?

THE BIG PICTURE

Population Growth Rate   Have you ever thought about what life will be like when you have your grandchildren on your knee and are boring them with tales about "the good old days"? Will day-to-day existence be so different in the future? Demographers estimate that the current global population of more than 5 billion people will double in about 50 years. In the United States, the human population is expected to double in roughly 100 years. In developing nations around the world, rapidly increasing populations put a strain on resources, especially on the ability to grow necessary food, the adequacy of housing, and the availability of clean water and health care.

The Quality of Life   The quality of life differs greatly from developing nations with a high population growth rate to the developed countries with a low population growth rate. A few developed countries, such as Denmark and Germany, are actually experiencing a decline in population. In many ways, a single family in a developed country has a greater environmental impact than a similarly-sized family from a developing nation. The family in the developed country probably eats more, buys more consumable goods, uses more electric power, and creates more trash. But that family also receives more education, enjoys better health, and has more leisure time than does a family in a developing country.

How does your community fit into the whole picture of global population? Is the population of your community increasing or decreasing? Are changes in the population affecting the quality of life where you live? Looking at population statistics can help you better understand how population and quality of life are related.

JUST DO IT

1. Gather population data about your own community. Your local board of education has probably conducted a census in your school district and will have adequate information about the students enrolled in your school district and about the general population. Ask your teacher to help you get this information. (Census information for your region has also been published by the Federal government and is available to you. See *Going Further* on page 24.)

2. Use these census data to make a population bar graph of your community, showing how many residents fit into each age group. The statistics themselves will give you an idea of how to create age groups. For example, a census may include how many pre-kindergarten children live in your district, how many students are enrolled in each grade, as well as the numbers of adults in the over-18 and in the over-65 age groups who are voters in your community.

3. If practical, calculate the average age of the members of your community and show that number on your graph. The average age is calculated by finding the sum of the ages of each person and dividing by the total number of people. You may also wish to find the mode of your population graph. The mode is the age that occurs with the greatest frequency in your population. There may be more than one mode.

4. Compare the number of people of various ages that live in your town. How would you characterize your community?

5. Does the source of information show population statistics from ten years ago? Compare the numbers between then and now. Has the population grown or has it decreased? By how much? If possible, make a line graph to show population change over time.
6. Do you think that the average age has shifted over ten years? Is your community getting older or younger?

DECISION MAKING

1. Have your school district officials projected what the future enrollment of your school will be? Find out what their projections are. Then compare them to your own data by extrapolating your statistics into the future.
2. Do you think that your community will become a crowded one? How do you think population changes may affect the quality of life in your community? How might they affect housing, education, sources of jobs, travel, and recreation?
3. How will increases in the size of the human population change the ecosystem in which you live?
4. What might be some factors limiting your community's growth?

GOING FURTHER

Do you live in a part of the country that has a high growth rate? Do you think that most people continue to live in the state in which they were born? Are people moving from other states to live in your state? To get detailed census information published by the Federal government, you will have to go to a library where such information is available. If your local public library does not have it, you may have to try a university or college library. To find out which library to go to, first call the Federal Information Center at 1-800-347-1997 and ask which regional U.S. Census Bureau office is nearest you. That office can tell you the local libraries that carry census information. A publication called CP1 (Census of Population 1) will contain the data you need. You may also be able to get a Profiles of Places printout to give you the census details of a particular community or region.

USING LAND WISELY

THE BIG PICTURE

Preserving the Land   People of the Lummi Nation have fished for salmon in the river rapids of the northwest United States for generations. These Native Americans have carved exquisite wooden ceremonial sculptures from the ancient trees of Washington state for hundreds of years. But, as other people settled the region, the expanding human population required more room for cities and towns, which in turn brought increases in logging and agriculture, manufacturing and commerce. To accommodate these needs, some people cut the great forests and scarred the land forever. Today members of the Lummi Nation speak of preservation for the land, for the fir trees, for the fish, for the birds. They often repeat a saying common to many Native Americans: *As keepers of the Earth, we are to preserve and respect the land for seven generations to come.* This way of thinking comes from a culture that lived in harmony with nature without thought of ownership and exploitation, a culture that worked toward maintaining a balance with nature so that one's great-grandchildren could experience the same clear streams, the same breathtaking mountain vistas.

Wisdom in Land Use   Preservation of the natural beauty of the wilderness was one important reason for the creation of national and state park lands. Today, although many parks remain undeveloped wilderness, some government-owned lands throughout the West have been opened up for mining, ranching, or logging, causing concern among those who seek to preserve the environment. Can the unspoiled beauty of nature be combined with the human need for land and resources? Yes, say some people in different parts of the country where entire communities have been planned and designed to stay in balance with nature rather than control it. In one community in Florida, houses and stores are clustered together, leaving plenty of open, undeveloped land and views of the sea. But planned communities are rare. Usually towns and cities grow in an unplanned, sprawling fashion, using up valuable farmland and forests. How can people plan for the future and strike a balance between preserving natural lands and maintaining a lifestyle suitable to contemporary society? Take a closer look at how land has been used in your own community over the years.

JUST DO IT

1. Plan an interview with someone who has lived in your community for an entire lifetime. Refer to the interview guidelines on page 26.
2. Using newspaper articles, personal anecdotes, photographs, or other memorabilia, put together a history of your community that emphasizes how the land has been used. Make two displays to contrast how things were with how things are now. For example, you might create two maps showing how land was used in the past and how it is used today. Shade each area in a different color according to land use. Categories might include residential housing, high-rise housing, schools, business districts, roads, factories, farmlands, grazing lands, parks, open space, and so on.
3. Prepare an oral report to accompany your presentation. Present it to your class and invite the people you have interviewed. You might explore the possibility of making your presentation at another location, such as a residence for senior citizens.

Guidelines for a Successful Interview

1. Choose a person with whom you have some kind of relationship or someone whom you think would be willing to participate.
2. Contact the person you are going to interview in advance with a phone call or a letter. State exactly what you plan to do.
3. Bring a notebook and/or tape recorder to the interview. Remember that it is always best to get names, places and dates in writing, as well as on tape. A tape recording may not be clear enough when you play it back.
4. Be prepared with thoughtful questions that you have written in advance. Go to the interview with those questions ready, but let the conversation be spontaneous.
5. Be aware that some senior citizens may have sight or hearing loss, or other limiting health conditions. Be considerate.
6. Be understanding, inquisitive, and show enthusiasm for what the person has done over a lifetime. Ask for funny anecdotes about how things used to be. Ask to see, or perhaps borrow, old photographs or newspaper articles, if possible. Make copies of them and return them to the owner.

DECISION MAKING

1. From the information you have gathered, make a projection about how land will be used in the future. Which of your land-use categories will probably increase in area? Which will decrease?
2. Suppose you are on the planning board of your town, and a developer is proposing a new shopping mall, housing development, or factory. Present your support or criticism of such a development and give your view of which sites would be most appropriate.
3. Suppose that there is some preserved land next to a wooded area that is cut for timber. The timber company wants to cut a road through the preserve to decrease the distance that the logs would have to travel to get to a mill. Using the present road takes a long time and the logging trucks waste fuel and pollute the air. Should the company get its road? Present both sides of the argument.
4. A preserved area is home to several endangered species of plants as well as a fast-growing deer population. Without predation, the deer may increase in number and begin to starve. The preserve is opened to deer hunters as a solution. Do you agree or disagree with that policy? Give reasons for your position.
5. Find out what the term "mixed use" of land might mean. Discuss.

GOING FURTHER

1. Does your county or town have a Landmarks Commission or Historical Society? Find out where and why certain areas or buildings are preserved.
2. Investigate the history of a national park nearest you. Is the government allowing any development there? Why? Do you think it is right?

SORTING IT OUT WITH RECYCLING

THE BIG PICTURE

Ways to Recycle Garbage Mountains of garbage stand as monuments to a nation of consumers accustomed to a lifestyle of using something once and throwing it away. But there is some good news. People are slowly learning the new "Three-R's": *reduce, reuse, and recycle.* Even a major fast-food chain jumped onto the recycling bandwagon by experimenting with recycled plastic foam food containers, trying to turn them into usable plastic products like yo-yos. However, that program was abandoned in favor of using paper wrapping instead of plastic foam and foil. Industry goals set for recycling cans and bottles have been met and surpassed in some places. The National Soft Drink Association reports that in 1991, 54 percent of all soft-drink cans and bottles were recycled through curbside pickup, central drop-off locations, and other programs, a higher percentage than expected.

In the last several years there have been other examples of a nation-wide move in the right direction. The town of Islip, New York received a lot of bad press in 1987 when a garbage barge loaded with Islip garbage sailed into countless ports in search of a place to dump its cargo, to no avail. Now the same community has something to cheer about—a state-of-the-art recycling facility that has greatly reduced the volume of its wastes.

Recycling and the Environment What does recycling really do for the environment? By reducing the need for new materials, recycling directly prevents pollution and the irreparable loss of precious natural resources. You can do your share of recycling if you think carefully about what you throw away every day. Start by taking a waste audit of your home and see just what it is that is going out with the trash.

RECYCLING DATA

Recycling one ton of steel:
- prevents 200 pounds of pollutants from entering the air
- prevents 100 pounds of pollutants from entering the water
- prevents 3 tons of waste at the mining site
- prevents the need for 25 tons of water for the steel-making process

Recycling one ton of aluminum:
- prevents the mining of 4 tons of bauxite ore
- prevents the need for a ton of fossil fuels and cuts energy use by 90 percent

Recycling 1 ton of paper:
- saves 17 trees, which can absorb 250 pounds of carbon dioxide a year
- prevents 1500 pounds of carbon dioxide caused by burning a ton of paper from entering the atmosphere

JUST DO IT

Part I Take an inventory of the garbage your household produces for one week. If that is impractical, do it for at least a day or two. Ask other members of your household to help. Each day, you will look at all the garbage that your household has produced, sort it out, and weigh it as carefully as you can. To take a home-waste audit, follow these steps.

1. Get an old carton, box, or storage crate, as well as a brown paper shopping bag. You will be using these two containers for storing items that are recyclable. You will also need a bathroom scale.

2. At the end of each day, place the household garbage bag on the bathroom scale and weigh the contents. (You may have to weigh yourself holding the bag and then subtract your weight alone from the total.) Keep a log of your data. Use the following model log.

Daily Household Waste by Weight

Day	Weight of Recyclables	Weight of Non-recyclables	Total Weight
1			
2			
3			
4			
5			
6			
7			
Totals			

Amount of Recyclables by Weight

Day	Newspaper	Glass	Plastic	Cans and Foil	Total
1					
2					
3					
4					
5					
6					
7					
Totals					

3. Separate out all the recyclable items: paper, glass, metal, and plastic. These items include newspapers, aluminum cans and foil, tin cans, glass containers, plastic soda and milk containers, and hard plastic containers such as laundry detergent bottles. Rinse out the containers. Weigh each group of recyclables and record the weights in your log.

4. Stack the newspapers and place them in the paper bag. Place the other recyclables in your recycling container.

5. Each day, take some time to examine the plastic containers to find the numbers stamped on them that indicate whether or not they should be recycled. Use the information in the box at the top of page 29 to help you sort them.

Plastics may not weigh very much, but they take up a lot of space in landfills. If they are incinerated, they produce toxic gases. Recyclable plastic is stamped with the "recyclable" logo, three connected arrows. You will find the stamp on the underside of plastic containers, usually with a number inside.

- Containers stamped "1" may also have the letters PET or PETE stamped on them. Soda bottles are made of this kind of plastic, which can be recycled and made into carpets, clothing, and fiberfill.
- Containers stamped "2" may also be marked HDPE. These sturdy plastic containers are recycled into trash cans, flower pots, traffic safety cones, and maybe even park benches.
- Containers stamped "3" are usually not recycled because of their chemical makeup. Those stamped "4" may be recycled into plastic bags or plastic film.

6. Take a look at the other garbage left behind. How much of it is waste paper such as wrapping from packages, cardboard, junk mail, or discarded school or office papers? Weigh this waste exactly or estimate its weight. Can you think of an alternative to throwing it all away? (Try cutting up some of the paper having writing on one side and make a memo pad.)

7. Approximate the weight of paper trash—towels, napkins, tissues, or disposable diapers. How much of this solid waste could be eliminated by using reusable cloth substitutes?

8. Approximate the weight of the other plastics in the garbage. Plastic wrap, plastic foam coffee cups, and fast-food containers are generally not recyclable. However, clean plastic shopping bags from your local supermarket may often be returned and recycled. Check on it.

9. Leftover food scraps may also make up a portion of your garbage. (Weighing them could be a rather messy undertaking. Just approximate.) Vegetable or fruit peelings are good for feeding small pets like guinea pigs or for adding to a compost pile.

10. You may have other items in the garbage, such as broken appliances, old clothes, or toys. Before tossing them, think of alternatives suggested by the Three-Rs. Can anything be fixed or given away?

Part II   When you have completed your waste audit, you should have a week's worth of data showing by weight what part of the household garbage was recyclable and what was not.

1. Total all your data. Then make a pie chart or pictograph to show your results.

2. Share your data with your class. Total the weight of all the recyclable and nonrecyclable garbage generated by everyone in the class. Use these figures to calculate the average amount of recyclable and nonrecyclable garbage generated per household. Make graphs to show the results.

3. Find out how many people live in your community. Calculate how much recyclable and nonrecyclable garbage is generated each week by your community.

DECISION MAKING

1. Now that you have a week's worth of recyclables, what are you going to do with them? How are these items recycled in your community?
   a. *Curbside collection of recyclables* Some communities provide curbside bins for collecting recyclables. If you are in such a community, make sure you actively participate. Officials in Seattle, Washington think that by the turn of the century curbside collection will help to reduce the waste stream by 50 percent.
   b. *Voluntary recycling centers* These centers may accept newspaper, cans, glass, and plastic, usually presorted by type and color. If this kind of facility is near you, help to arrange with neighbors or friends to bring recyclables to the facility regularly.
   c. *Recycling in the planning stage* Are there plans for recycling in your community? If there is not, help to organize a recycling effort.
2. In one city in the Northwest, people were being charged per garbage can for garbage pickup, as a way to reduce the amount of community garbage. Soon, people started compacting their trash so that they would need fewer cans. In response, the city began weighing the garbage and charging people by weight. Garbage was sorted by weight. Is volume a better way to measure garbage than weight? Discuss this issue with your classmates.
3. Is your school cafeteria using all throwaway containers? Calculate the number and volume of containers generated over a month. Think of alternatives for your school. Students can make a difference. In a New Jersey town, students were upset when the school board wanted to use cheap, disposable plastic trays in the cafeteria. Students said they would be willing to pay a few cents more for lunch on a biodegradable cardboard tray. The board made the switch to cardboard. If you have useful suggestions for more environmentally correct practices in your school, put your suggestions in a polite, intelligent letter to school officials.

GOING FURTHER

1. Try making something out of recycled materials. Make a recycled toy, game, or gift for someone. One idea is to create your own version of indoor basketball. Cut out a hole near the top of a large plastic detergent bottle. hang the bottle from a doorknob or a hook to make a hoop. Fill an old sock with dried beans and sew it closed. Make a game of tossing the bean bag through the hoop.
2. Find out where your garbage goes when it leaves your home. Landfills are closing at an alarming rate because they are full. Does your town pay to haul your garbage off to another state? Is your garbage burned and becoming a source of air pollution? Write a short report of your findings.
3. Paper is often claimed to be a better alternative to plastic containers because it is biodegradable—it is thought to decompose if it is dumped in a landfill. But even natural cellulose fibers need sunlight and air in order to decompose. Some people who routinely go through garbage dumps say they can still read 40-year-old newspapers. Design your own experiment to compare the degree of biodegradability of different packaging materials.

GOING, GOING, GONE: ENDANGERMENT AND EXTINCTION

THE BIG PICTURE

We often hear that because there are as many as 700 000 minke whales, killing just 300 of them every year will have no effect on the overall population. However, when we look beyond the numbers, and recognize, from a social science perspective, that these creatures have a deep relationship with human beings, this becomes a dangerous way of thinking.

—Eiji Fujiwara, President of the Institute for Environmental Science and Culture in Japan

Disappearing Species There are about 1.5 million identified species of plants and animals on this planet, and there are as many as 30 million more that have never been identified, never even been seen by human eyes. Why is there such concern for the loss or extinction of species? Answering this question means taking a look at the balance of nature. The organisms on this planet are always evolving, changing over time. Some species, like the dinosaurs, became extinct because of natural processes. But today the loss of species is thousands of times greater because of human activity. By the turn of the twenty-first century, some experts estimate that a tenth of all species will be lost. The reasons are numerous. As human populations increase, the habitats of animals are encroached upon and changed forever. Overfishing the oceans completely wipes out species that are unable to reproduce fast enough to keep up with the catch. The loss affects other organisms above them in the food chain. Huge areas given over to agriculture eliminate the natural habitat of native plants.

When a plant becomes extinct, some experts claim that it can begin a chain reaction, causing thirty other dependent organisms to move closer to extinction.

The beauty of nature lies in its incredible diversity. Every species contributes something unique to its environment, bringing with it its own characteristics and genetic makeup. Around the globe, perhaps from fifty to one hundred species become extinct each day—some of them never seen nor identified. Which one of them could have been an important food source or potential source of drugs that could have saved human life? There is no way of knowing after they become extinct.

Saving Endangered Species In 1973, the Endangered Species Act was passed in the United States to slow down the extinction process, and a number of successful programs were begun. Animals such as the peregrine falcon and the whooping crane were brought back from near extinction by programs of captive breeding. Since that time, the government has been at work trying to keep track of animals and plants that are either near extinction or threatened with extinction. The United States Fish and Wildlife Service lists almost 600 species of animals and plants as endangered—in danger of extinction. Another 200 are threatened—very close to endangerment. And, some preservationists maintain that many other species that belong on one list or the other have just been missed.

JUST DO IT

The list on the next page shows the number of endangered species in the United States, state by state. This number is constantly changing. Usually more new species are added. Sometimes the same animal or plant is listed in more than one state. For example, the symbol of the United States, the bald eagle, is listed as endangered in 44 states.

AL	70	HI	126	MA	17	NM	34	SD	10
AK	6	ID	9	MI	16	NY	20	TN	60
AZ	45	IL	23	MN	11	NC	47	TX	64
AR	20	IN	17	MS	31	ND	9	UT	35
CA	110	IA	15	MO	22	OH	13	VT	10
CO	26	KS	15	MT	10	OK	18	VA	50
CT	13	KY	34	NE	12	OR	23	WA	16
DE	12	LA	21	NV	34	PA	11	WV	18
FL	83	ME	9	NH	8	RI	13	WI	14
GA	41	MD	21	NJ	15	SC	32	WY	11

1. Looking at the list, which states have the greatest number of endangered species? Which have the smallest numbers? Why do you think this is so? The answers could be different for different states.

2. Find your state. How many endangered species are there? Are you aware of any of the endangered plants and animals that live in your state? Do some research to find out what they are.

3. Many conservation biologists believe that in order to save a species, people must concentrate on saving the habitat in which that species lives. Prepare a brief report or make a model of the kind of habitat where an endangered species from your state would be found. Is there an attempt being made to save that habitat?

DECISION MAKING

1. Captive breeding programs involve capturing some of the few remaining animals of a species, allowing them to breed in captivity, and then returning them to their natural habitat. What are some pros and cons of such a program? Do you think that it is right to take animals from their natural habitat for breeding purposes?

2. The spotted owl is an endangered bird whose habitat is the old growth forest of the Northwest. This ancient forest represents the last five percent of the virgin forests that once existed in the United States. Logging in the Pacific Northwest continues in areas that are part of a national forest. The issue has polarized environmentalists, who wish to see logging halted, and loggers, who wish to preserve their livelihood. This issue has been so heated and emotional that even presidential policy is involved. Take a point of view on this issue. Do some research to prepare for a round-table discussion. Find out what other species besides the spotted owl are endangered by the felling of these old growth forests.

GOING FURTHER

To find out more about endangered species in the United States, you can write away for a catalogue that includes a complete list of endangered wildlife and plants and a copy of the Endangered Species Act of 1973. Write to: General Interest Publications, U.S. Fish and Wildlife Service, Publications Unit, 130 Webb Building, 4401 N. Fairfax Drive, Arlington, VA 22203.

SHARING THE WORLD WITH WILDLIFE

THE BIG PICTURE

Native American Wisdom About Nature   The story below is from the Abenaki nation, Native Americans who lived in the woodlands of the Northeast 1000 years ago.

After Tabaldak made human beings, he dusted his hands and that dust fell to Earth. From that leftover dust Gluscabi created himself. He just sat up on the Earth and said to Tabaldak, "Here I am." Gluscabi was not as powerful as Tabaldak, but he sometimes tried to change things, as did his grandchildren, the human beings.

One day Gluscabi went into the woods to hunt with his bow and arrow. But the animals saw him coming and hid from him. Gluscabi unhappily returned home to the little lodge by the big water where his Grandmother Woodchuck was awaiting his return. "Grandmother," said Gluscabi, "Please make me a game bag to take, the next time I go hunting. All the animals I shall catch will be placed in it." So Grandmother Woodchuck wove him a bag of caribou hair. But Gluscabi said it was not good enough and he wanted another. Grandmother wove a finer, larger game bag of deer hair. Still Gluscabi was not pleased. Grandmother wove yet another game bag, this time of moose hair and porcupine quills. Gluscabi threw it to the ground and demanded another even better game bag. So Grandmother Woodchuck made him a magical game bag of woodchuck hair, pulling out the hair from her own belly. (Look at the belly of a woodchuck and you will see that there is still no hair there.) Gluscabi looked up at Grandmother and said, "*Oleohneh*" (Thank you).

Now when Gluscabi went back to the woods, he brought the game bag, but he did not need his bow and arrow. He called out to all the animals in the woodland and shouted to them that the world was about to be destroyed. To be saved, they should all jump into his game bag. And all the frightened animals jumped in, the rabbits and the squirrels, the raccoons and the foxes. Grandmother had not made him any ordinary game bag. The magic game bag grew larger and larger and there still was room for more animals. The deer, the caribou, the moose, and the bear all piled into the game bag as it stretched wider and wider. When all the animals were captured, Gluscabi tied the bag closed and gave out a big laugh. He slung the bag over his shoulder and returned home to Grandmother Woodchuck.

"Grandmother! Grandmother!" he exclaimed. "We will never have to do the hard work of hunting again."

As Grandmother opened the bag and saw all the animals of the world, she looked up at Gluscabi and said, "You cannot keep all the animals of the world in a game bag. They will get sick and die. There will be none left for your grandchildren's grandchildren. It is right that it is difficult to hunt. The animals stay stronger and wiser to avoid being caught, and you have have to be stronger and wiser to catch the ones that you need. Then things will be in the right balance."

Gluscabi went back to the woods. He told the animals that the world had been destroyed but he had put it back together again. So because Gluscabi listened to his grandmother, the animals came back out into the world, where they remain to this day.

This Native American story gives some insight to the view held by many native cultures—that human beings must not control the animals around them but live in harmony with them.

Myths abound in every culture around the globe in which people have been curious about the natural world. Stories have been passed down from generations long ago when people lived in balance with nature. Although our modern lives place value on material and technological advances, and native folklore may seem naive and unscientific, there is still much to be learned about how we can share the planet with all its wildlife.

Native Americans shared this continent with the deer, the buffalo, the salmon, and many other species. Hunting was an honor that began with a ceremony of giving thanks to the animals whose lives would be taken. Every part of a slaughtered animal was used, its meat for food, its skin for clothing or teepees, its antler and horn for tools and weapons. Wasting any part of an animal showed disrespect for living things.

In India today there is a Hindu sect, the Bishnois, that has protected desert plants and animals for hundreds of years. This sect has prevented hunters from killing animals and loggers from cutting down trees. Because of the vigilance of the Bishnois and in spite of the harsh, arid climate, there are groves of trees that have thrived for more than 500 years. And animals such as deer, peacocks, rabbits, and pigeons move about freely, unafraid of humans.

Methods of Wildlife Management   It is with more understanding that wildlife management has taken on a different tone in recent years. The stated goal of some wildlife management programs is to manage animal populations for the enjoyment and benefit of people without endangering the animals themselves. Wildlife biologists and technicians compile data on the number and types of indigenous animal populations by tagging and banding them to keep track of migratory patterns. Wildlife bureaus establish hunting, trapping, and fishing laws that will keep animal populations at healthy levels. They issue licenses to wildlife rehabilitators who can take care of distressed and injured animals. Most state or regional wildlife agencies have special programs for endangered species. Biologists must also deal with damage or other problems that occur when human and animal populations share a habitat. The biologists' aim is to strike a delicate balance to meet the needs of both human and animal populations.

JUST DO IT

1. Using reference materials such as books, magazines, or videotapes, do some research on animals that appear in myths, folklore, legends, literature, art, film, or plays. You might narrow your research to one culture, one that is appealing and interesting to you. Then select an animal.
2. Using scientific references, learn all you can about this animal scientifically—its species, classification, anatomy, physical characteristics, habitat, eating habits, and life cycle.
3. Integrate and synthesize what you have learned about your chosen animal to create an original presentation in an artistic medium. Use the activity list below for some options, or think of your own. You might want to work on your presentation with a group of classmates.

Sharing the World with Wildlife—Activity Options
- Create an animal mask in the tradition of another culture, using whatever materials are available to you.

- Carve or cast an animal totem.
- Use natural materials such as a gourd, wood, or animal hide to make a ceremonial object, perhaps a rattle or drum, to represent the animal in the Native American tradition.
- Draw or paint the animal.
- Find a myth or story that you really like, rewrite it in your own words, then illustrate it.
- Write your own modern adventure story that involves animals.
- Find a story that you would like to tell others in the tradition of good storytelling, perhaps using props to help the story along.
- Write and present a play that dramatizes an animal myth, using props and animal costumes.
- Do some research to find a native song or chant about animals and teach it to others.
- Write and perform an original song about animals, perhaps with accompaniment played on a native instrument.
- Create costumes and choreograph a dance to symbolize your animal.
- Make a video about the life cycle of an animal. Go to its habitat and film the video from the animal's point of view.

DECISION MAKING

1. What animal did you choose? Does the experience of doing something creative change or enhance your views about sharing the planet with wildlife?
2. Do you think it is right for people to keep exotic pets that come from other parts of the world? Explain your viewpoint.
3. What would you do if you found an injured animal? Would you keep it and try to nurse it back to health? Give suggestions.
4. Some wildlife conservationists support the doctrine of *sustainable utilization,* which allows "wise and rational" use of resources. What do you think permissible uses of wildlife would be? Should wildlife be used to promote tourism, especially in third-world countries? Should some elephants be killed for their ivory, or some leopards for their skins, so that native populations can raise money for their needs and for conservation programs? What are the possible pros and cons of such an approach?
5. Freqently, there are complaints from people who live in cities about sanitary problems caused by pigeons. Do some research on pigeons, the problem(s) they have caused, and some of the solutions that have been proposed. Do you think it is possible to solve the problems in a way that will allow human beings to continue sharing the planet with this form of wildlife?
6. The shark has often been portrayed as the terrible villain of the sea in novels and movies. But during the past decade, this fierce hunter has become the hunted. Scientists fear that, as a result of sharp declines in shark populations, the marine food web will be seriously, if not catastrophically, disturbed. Do some reaserach to find out what, if any, controls have been placed on shark fishing. Do you think the existing controls are adequate? What benefits that sharks might provide could be lost if shark fishing were to continue unchecked?

7. According to some biologists, the popularity of the panda in North American zoos has created a problem for the future survivial of these animals in the wild. Do some reasearch to find out about the effects on wild pandas of China's panda loans to American zoos. Discuss what is being done to promote preservation of pandas in the wild and whether or not these measures seem adequate.

GOING FURTHER

1. Expand your presentation so it can be shown to your school or community.
2. Visit a wildlife rehabilitation center or ask a wildlife rehabilitator to come to your school. Find out what the goal of rehabilitation is.
3. Visit a zoo or wild animal park. Rather than keeping animals in cages in a zoo (perhaps a modern-day game bag), animals are found roaming in natural settings of game parks. Ask zoo guides how exhibits and the philosophy of zoo management have changed.

THANK A TREE

THE BIG PICTURE

Other holidays repose upon the past.
Arbor Day proposes for the future.
—J. Sterling Morton
Founder of Arbor Day, 1872

Life-giving Trees   Plant a tree. Hug a tree. Thank a tree. What do all of these slogans have to do with the environment? Trees provide cooling shade in the heat of summer, habitats for animals, and root systems that hold precious soil. Many of the world's biomes are described by the number and kinds of trees that dominate the ecosystem. Every tree is a food factory, taking in carbon dioxide from the air and converting it to carbon-based sugars in its leaves and releasing oxygen produced during the process of photosynthesis. As tree leaves draw carbon dioxide from the air to manufacture food, they remove some of the greenhouse gas that contributes to global warming. In one year a single tree converts the amount of carbon dioxide that a car produces if it is driven for 26 000 miles. That same tree in one day produces enough oxygen for 18 people to breathe.

Programs for Planting Trees   The possibility of global warming was something Andy Lipkis heard about when he was still a teenager in the late 1960s. Thinking about how trees use carbon dioxide and reduce the amount of the greenhouse gases produced by pollution, he asked officials at his summer camp if they would tear up a parking lot and plant trees instead. At first, officials told him no, but after a while they agreed and trees were planted. As a college student with little money of his own, Andy called newspapers, politicians, and government agencies, convincing people to donate tree seedlings, as well as the labor needed to plant them. Soon a nonprofit organization called the TreePeople was born. Although exact numbers are unknown, millions of trees were planted in the Los Angeles area of California alone. Then, to support the American Forestry Association's quest to break up heat islands in cities, the TreePeople planted millions of trees in other cities in the United States. Soon similar organizations grew in other countries. Today, because of Andy Lipkis' concern for the environment, an ongoing project known as Global Releaf is taking place in many regions around the world.

JUST DO IT

What are some of the ways in which trees benefit you and your environment? In this activity you can take a census of nearby trees and estimate how much the trees help to alleviate the greenhouse effect in your community.

1. Take a census of trees by counting the number of trees in a given area. It could be on school grounds, in a park, or in your own yard. Make sure you have permission, if necessary.
2. Use a tape measure to mark off the area in which you are taking the census. The size of the area can vary, but keep it practical.
3. Make a map to scale on a piece of graph paper. As you count each tree in your census area, locate its position and mark it on the graph paper. If you know what kind of tree it is, label it and, if possible, measure the diameter of the tree and note that as well.

4. Approximate the age of the tree and note that on the map. Find out when the trees were planted. Look for fallen trees in the area and count their annual rings. This will help give you an idea of the ages of trees in your census area.
5. When you have counted all the trees, calculate the potential amount of carbon dioxide absorbed by each tree annually. Figures vary significantly, but it is safe to say that an entire acre of trees has the potential to absorb several tons of carbon dioxide every year. To find the amount absorbed by each tree, use this equation:

Carbon dioxide intake in pounds per year = $4.3 \times$ tree age $- 70$

6. Total the amount of carbon dioxide converted in your census area. Compare your total amount to these figures: In one year one home heated with oil releases 6.5 tons of carbon dioxide. Each car in the United States emits approximately 5 tons (10 000 pounds) of carbon dioxide per year.

DECISION MAKING

1. Discuss how trees planted help to counter the greenhouse effect. Should more trees be planted? Where should the funds for tree-planting come from?
2. What are some of the other benefits of having trees in your environment?
3. Studies show that during the summer a tree-lined neighborhood in a city can be several degrees cooler than streets with no trees. With air conditioners running less, the community can save thousands of kilowatt hours of electricity. Suppose you wanted to plant trees near your home to cut down on air conditioning costs. Where would you plant them?
4. How can cut trees, such as Christmas trees, be recycled and used to hold back erosion? Is there a program in your community for this use?

GOING FURTHER

Make suggestions to your school for planting trees on Arbor Day, the last Friday in April. Keep in mind that planting is easy, but caring for young saplings takes commitment and work.

How to Plant a Tree for a Cooler, Cleaner World

1. Locate a clear, open site for your tree, with generous rooting area and good drainage.
2. Loosen and clear the soil in the entire planting area 6 to 10 inches deep. In the center, dig a hole at least as wide, but only as deep as the root ball.
3. Remove tree from burlap or container and place on solidly packed soil so that the root collar (where the tree's main stem meets the roots) is slightly above the surrounding grade.
4. Backfill the hole and lightly pack the soil into place around the tree.
5. Spread a 2- to 3-inch deep layer of mulch in the entire area, for a distance of 6 to 8 inches around the tree trunk.
6. Stake the tree so that it can flex in the wind. Attach stake to the tree by using discarded rubber inner-tubes. Remove them after six months.
7. Water thoroughly, but do not flood the hole. Water twice a week during dry periods.

THE RAIN FOREST

THE BIG PICTURE

Our principal line of action is the defense of our land and our resources, as well as our right to our own language, culture, and education, to self-determination and political representation for the security of our people.

—Evaristo Nugkuag, member of the Aguarunan tribe of Peru, Founder of the Coordinating Organization for Indigenous Bodies in the Amazon Basin

What do you see when you think of the rain forest? Do you picture colorful toucans and brightly-hued frogs hopping within the lush canopy of green trees? Do you see clouds of steamy moisture rising from the dense vegetation? Perhaps you also see animals fleeing the approach of earth-moving machines cutting a swath through the ancient trees.

Biological Diversity of the Rain Forest The biological diversity of the rain forest is without comparison. The rain forest, which covers only six percent of Earth's surface, is home to well over half of all species on the planet. As the rain forests diminish in size each day, environmentalists are most troubled by fifteen hot spots, tropical forests in which biodiversity is especially at risk. These hot spots make up a little over ten percent of all tropical forests, but may contain one-third to one-half of all the world's plant species.

Not only do these plants and animals represent a breathtaking array of colorful life forms, but they include species that have potential uses as new food sources to feed the hungry or as sources of drugs that can cure the world's

diseases. From Madagascar, the island nation off the coast of Africa, the Madagascar periwinkle has been used as the basis of a drug to fight leukemia and Hodgkin's disease. The rain forest of Madagascar is quickly disappearing under the constant pressure of a growing population that needs land. A tree in the Amazon produces a sap that is very similar to diesel oil—so much so that it can be poured into a fuel tank and used by trucks. A weevil from the rain forest of Cameroon has successfully been brought to Malaysia where it pollinates the oil-palm trees, saving plantation owners millions of dollars annually. Each of these species could easily have been overlooked or brought to the point of extinction by the devastation of rain forests worldwide.

Stopping Deforestation Developing nations with a need for land have cut rain forests for lumber and burned lands to make way for agriculture and ranching. However, the agricultural gains last only a few years because, for all the biological wealth of the rain forest, the soil is actually poor in nutrients. Farming the land for only a few years depletes these nutrients. However, global awareness of the plight of the rain forest is aiding indigenous people to move closer toward a stable management policy of the rain forest. New products coming to the global marketplace from the rain forest use renewable resources such as fruits, nuts, oil, and gums rather than wood, which requires destruction of the trees. In this way the people who live in the rain forest can enjoy long-term economic gain while preserving biodiversity of species.

JUST DO IT

The way you can best aid the rain forest is by supporting an economy that values rather than exploits its diversity. Investigate the world of rain-forest related products.

1. Visit several stores in your community including gift shops, department stores,

clothing stores, home furnishing outlets, furniture stores, gourmet food shops, florists, and pet shops. Go prepared with a notebook.

2. Take a survey of all the available products that you think come from the rain forest. Examine the labels. Ask store clerks. Find out what kinds of materials go into each product. Use the lists below to guide you.

Rain forest animals sometimes illegally captured and found in exotic pet shops:
macaws	cockatoos	monkeys	ocelots
pythons	boa constrictors	iguanas	

Tropical plants that may be taken from the rain forest and sold in florist shops:
rare bromeliads   rare orchids

Tropical woods that may be used in home furnishings (furniture, bowls, sculptures)
teak	mahogany	rosewood	ebony

Renewable forest resources that promote management of rain forests:
fruits	nuts	oils
flowers	rubber	resins

3. Compile two lists of products, those that help to support the rain forest and those that further its destruction.
4. Do you find any products that state what percentage of profits made from selling the product go to promoting proper management of the rain forest? If you can, bring in some of these products to school. (They may be good food, such as Brazil nuts, to share!)

DECISION MAKING

1. Suppose you own an import-export business and are attending an international trade fair. You meet a manufacturer of beautiful teakwood tables and the president of a small company that manufactures skin lotion made from plant extract. Which person would you rather help find a market? How would your decision be affected if you could make a lot more money selling high-priced teak furniture?
2. Suppose you are hired by a pharmaceutical company to collect plant extracts from bromeliads, plants high up in the rain forest canopy. The company hopes to test the extracts for potential use as drugs to cure disease. Upon your arrival you find that a mining company is planning to build a road in the same area. What would you do?
3. How would you persuade someone that global deforestation and the greenhouse effect are related?

GOING FURTHER

Use reference books or magazines to research the biodiversity of a rain forest. Choose several plants or animals that you feel represent the plight of the shrinking rain forest. Use them to prepare a display that communicates the need for halting deforestation.

WHY ARE WETLANDS IMPORTANT?

THE BIG PICTURE

Some farmers in Virginia knew that there was good timber out in that gloomy swamp, but the ground was just too soggy for them to cut down the trees. They decided to drain the wetland, which was fittingly named Dismal Swamp. One of the engineers of the plan was a surveyor named George Washington. Today, Dismal Swamp is a protected park that symbolizes the many wet, soggy, mosquito-infested "wastelands" that were drained throughout the eighteenth and nineteenth centuries as the Atlantic coast was settled. Even in this century, such lands were drained to create harbors, make room for coastal development, or eradicate the habitats of insect pests. While those programs seemed like good ideas at the time, scientists recently have learned of the value of wetlands.

Characteristics of Wetlands   A wetland is a transitional area between land and a deepwater habitat, such as an ocean or large freshwater lake. Scientists recognize several types of wetlands. Marine wetlands occur along the coast and along estuaries, where rivers meet the ocean. Freshwater wetlands occur near lakes, rivers, and streams and include swamps and bogs. Wetlands are among the most productive of all environments. For example, a single acre of cattail marsh can produce 12 tons of biomass in a year. Cattails, commonly found in wetlands, are tall plants with their roots in water. Such plants are called emergents. Other kinds of wetland vegetation include floating islands of lilies, mosses, and algae, as well as other plants that stay submerged in the water. Plant diversity allows for very complex food webs that begin with either water or terrestrial plants. Wetland habitats serve as nurseries for many species of water birds and amphibians, and are home to many endangered species.

Hidden within tall marsh grass, a female bird can build a nest and lay her eggs. The shallow water is rich with nutrients, and the lack of a strong current makes for a calm, protected refuge for young, flightless birds.

Wetlands also serve as a buffer for neighboring ecosystems. The porous soil holds water after a rainfall, reducing flooding in nearby locations. When pollutants enter underground water, they become diluted in the existing water. The meadowlands of New Jersey, salt marshes across the Hudson River from New York City, are mainly undeveloped acres of marsh grasses. Yet underneath the waving grass, the ground is constantly absorbing and filtering many of the pollutants from urban runoff.

Interfering with the Balance   Wetlands are home to populations of algae and blue-green bacteria, which are sensitive to the amount of organic nutrients in the shallow water. As a result, these areas may experience periodic blooms in which vast numbers of these organisms proliferate. Blooms are natural phenomena that are often stimulated by runoff containing fertilizers and detergents. Phosphates and nitrates from these products provide additional nutrients to the water. As a result, millions of tiny organisms grow at once, creating great floating masses. When they begin to die, the mass of organic matter decays, robbing the shallow water of precious oxygen. Marshes, however, contain other bacteria that can switch to anaerobic cell processes to obtain energy when there is an oxygen deficit. Although the methane gas released during these processes makes the marshes rather foul-smelling, it is evidence that the organisms of these unique habitats can maintain an ecological balance under varying conditions.

JUST DO IT

Part I   In this part of the activity, you can see the effects of nutrients on the growth of wetland organisms.

1. Obtain algae from a pond or from a stock culture. A good choice is *Spirogyra,* a common green filamentous alga that is easy to grow and observe.

2. Blot the algae on paper towels. Weigh out 5-gram pieces of the algae and place them into four separate beakers each half full of pond water. Three beakers will be experimental. Leave one for a control.

3. To each experimental beaker, add a different solution made with 1 gram of a detergent dissolved in 99 grams of water (a 1% solution). Use three different detergents, including at least one that contains phosphates and one that does not contain phosphates. Add distilled water to the control beaker. Fill each beaker to the 3/4 mark.

4. Label the beakers appropriately. Cover them loosely with plastic wrap and place the beakers where they will get equal amounts of sunlight.

5. Observe the beakers each day and record your observations. Bubbles indicate release of gas during photosynthesis.

6. At the end of a week, remove the algae from each beaker, blot dry and weigh. Observe any changes in mass. Which beaker showed the greatest amount of growth? What can you conclude about the presence of phosphates in pond water?

Part II   In this part of the activity, you will take a field trip to a wetland.

1. Find out which type of wetland is found in your area. If you live along the coast, there may be tidal marshes, salt marshes, or estuaries. In inland areas, there are many freshwater wetlands, formed after the Ice Ages, that are home to many migrating waterfowl.

2. Plan a visit to such a wetland. What are the dominant species of plants there? Divide them into two categories, emergent plants and submerged plants. What are the dominant animals? Find out if there are any endangered species.

3. Has there been bloom in this wetland recently? How can you tell?

DECISION MAKING

Suppose a wetland near your home is being drained to make way for a housing development. Would you be in favor of or opposed to such development? What kinds of data would you want to have before making an informed decision?

GOING FURTHER

Is your class interested in preserving or maintaining a wetland? Some states have programs known as Adopt-a-Wetland. Contact your regional conservation department to find out whether a wetlands program exists in your area.

BALANCING ACT

THE BIG PICTURE

Relationships Within an Ecosystem In every ecosystem there is a relationship between the *abiotic* factors (physical aspects of the environment) and the *biotic* factors (relationships among organisms). An ecosystem with little rainfall and warm annual temperatures has a living community made up of animals and plants adapted to that climate. By contrast, a wet marsh with seasonal temperature differences has its own unique balance of producers, herbivores, and carnivores that form its pyramid of energy.

Two different ecosystems Compare the sketches on this page and the next, one of a desert community, the other, of a wet marsh community. Study the sketches carefully and compare the organisms shown in these very different ecosystems. What producers are pictured in each of these ecosystems? What consumers do you see in each? Which consumers do you think are at the top of the food chain in each community? In what ways is the ecosystem where you live different from or similar to either of these two?

Desert

Herbivore — Mule deer

Red tail hawk

Carnivores

King snake

Herbivore — Swallowtail butterfly

Producer — Saguaro cactus

Collared lizard

Carnivore

White footed mouse — Herbivore

Kangaroo rat — Herbivore

Kit fox — Carnivore

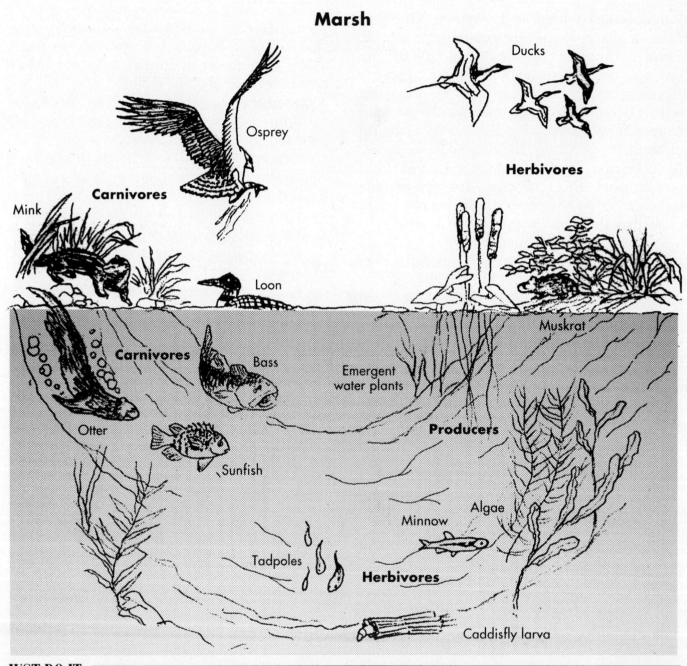

Marsh

JUST DO IT

How do all the pieces come together in a balanced ecosystem? Do an in-depth survey of a local ecosystem. Choose an environmental site for study. It can be a favorite wooded area, a park, a pond, or part of a wetland within a city. Get permission to visit the site several times to gather data.

Part I   First take a survey of the biotic factors of your site.

1. Work with your group to mark off a square 10 meters on a side, using a meter stick or tape measure.

2. Use a mallet to drive a stake into each of the four corners. Loop some string around each stake to form a square.

3. Take a survey of the plants you observe within the square. Use a plant key or guide book to help you learn the names of the plant species you observe. Write the plant names in a chart which includes the headings shown below.

PLANT SURVEY

Woody plants
tall trees
understory trees
saplings
shrubs
tree seedlings

Ground cover
mosses
lichens

Herbaceous plants
grasses
flowering plants

Water plants
emergent
submerged
floating

4. You may wish to further divide the square into smaller squares, each one meter on a side. Individual students can concentrate on the plants in their smaller squares and determine which plant species are the most dominant.

5. On the next visit, observe all the animals that enter and leave the site. Write down your observations according to the headings shown below.

Vertebrates
mammals
birds
reptiles
amphibians
fish

Invertebrates
segmented worms
mollusks
insects
crustaceans
spiders

6. Determine if the animals you observe are herbivores or carnivores. Write some sample food chains or food webs that might exist in the ecosystem. Place the names of species in a pyramid of energy and determine the dominant species at each trophic level.

7. Find out if there are any ecologically sensitive or endangered organisms.

Part II Take a survey of the abiotic factors of your site.

1. Use almanacs or other sources to determine the yearly temperature and rainfall of your site. If possible, place weather gauges on the site and collect weather data for several weeks.

2. Make graphs of yearly temperature and rainfall.

3. Determine the source of the ecosystem's water. Analyze it by using pH paper to determine the pH. Is it acid, basic, or neutral?

4. Are there sources of pollution entering the groundwater? If so, list them.

5. Describe any seasonal differences you observe in the water supply. Does the water dry up in the summer or ice over in winter?

6. What is the soil like? What is its pH? Is it high in humus, clay, or sand content?

Part III Round out your detailed profile of the environmental site.
1. Take photographs of the site or videotape it during different kinds of weather conditions.
2. Determine the factors which make this site unique. Write a cohesive description of the site in several paragraphs.

DECISION MAKING

1. Suppose you are applying for a grant to preserve the environmental site that you have just profiled. Outline what you would say during a presentation and how you would use your data to show how unique the site is.
2. Suppose someone wants to develop this site and build a housing and shopping complex there. Explain in writing how development would affect the unique ecological balance of plants and animals at the site. What you write is similar to an environmental impact statement (EIS), which is required whenever a proposal is made to develop an ecologically sensitive area.
3. Is there a parcel of land in your community over which there is current dispute as to whether or not it should be developed? Collect articles and letters to the editor that people have written about this local issue. Which side do you take? Justify your position.

GOING FURTHER

Is the environmental site that you studied situated on land that is already preserved or it is possible that someday it will be paved over and developed? Learn how to write a good letter to your local officials, newspaper editors, or representatives in Congress about doing something to save or preserve an area. Choose a real issue and practice writing a letter, using the guidelines below.
• Always address the letter formally and be sure of the correct spelling of proper titles and addresses.
• In your first paragraph always state clearly what you are writing about. Focus on one subject per letter. If you are writing to an elected official, state what you are asking that official to do—introduce a bill, vote for a bill, and so on. If you know of a specific bill, give its appropriate number. In writing a letter to the editor of a newspaper, briefly state the issue and your concern. Keep your tone courteous.
• In the second and third paragraphs, further explain your point of view or state the reasons why you want an elected official to take your position. Give evidence to support your position or a brief description of any research you have done.
• In your final paragraph, write a brief summary of what you are asking for. Try to keep the letter to one page. Type it or write in very legible handwriting. Keep a copy of the letter for future reference.

BE AN EARTHWISE CONSUMER

THE BIG PICTURE

Every day, Americans buy millions of dollars worth of food, detergents, bleaches, cleaning products, school supplies, paper products, personal care products, garden supplies, baby diapers, trash bags, and pet supplies. Most of these products are purchased by consumer choice. Can they also be purchased with an eye toward the safety of the environment?

Buying Green   Not all products are created equal. Some cleaning agents contain hazardous chemicals that find their way into the water supply. Some personal care products cause air pollution. Many disposable products have nonbiodegradable packaging that has the potential to remain in landfills for thousands of years. By choosing products that reduce pollution and are packaged in biodegradable materials, consumers send a powerful message to manufacturers that the environment is important. This trend toward more environmentally-sound products is sometimes called *buying green*, the color that represents the natural environment. But people sometimes find it difficult to break their buying habits. What are some of your buying habits? Are you ready to be an Earthwise consumer?

JUST DO IT

In this activity, you can compile a list of environmentally sound products that you or your family can use at home or at school.

1. Make a typical shopping list of the kinds of things that you or your family buy. Use these categories: *food, paper products, cleaning products, personal care products.*
2. Find which specific brand names of each product are the least harmful to the environment, using the characteristics given below. Then, next to each item, write some of the brand names that you might choose because they meet one or more of these criteria. You might also write in red some favorite products that don't meet these standards.

FOOD:
   Breakfast:
      eggs: in cardboard rather than Styrofoam box
      cereal: in recycled or recyclable cardboard box
      coffee filters: unbleached
   Lunch:
      drinks: recyclable cans or bottles
      snacks, meats, cheese: buy in large quantities rather than in
         single-servings with lots of packaging
   Dinner:
      loose fruits and vegetables rather than prepackaged
      recycled or recyclable cardboard boxes rather than plastic packaging
   For all foods:
      look for pesticide-free, additive-free, preservative-free foods
      recycled or recyclable packaging

PAPER PRODUCTS:
> waxed paper instead of plastic wrap
> paper towels purchased sparingly
> *For all paper products:*
> look for recyclable, recycled, biodegradable, unbleached or
> dioxin-free, dye-free, unscented products

CLEANING PRODUCTS (LAUNDRY, KITCHEN, BATHROOM):
> avoid aerosol oven cleaner with lye, drain openers, air fresheners,
> floor polishes, moth balls
> toilet bowl cleaners: hydrochloric acid or calcium hypochlorite are
> not really polluters; avoid paradichlorobenzene, which is toxic.
> *For all cleaners:*
> look for phosphate-free, chlorine-free, dye-free, unscented products;
> recycled packaging.

PERSONAL CARE PRODUCTS:
> hairspray: use pump, not aerosol (even though CFCs are banned,
> propellants in aerosols still contribute to smog)
> shaving products: avoid disposable razors; use electric when possible
> shaving cream, shampoo, conditioners: formaldehyde free
> first-aid products and drugs: use cardboard rather than metal or
> plastic packaging
> *For all personal care products:*
> look for synthetic chemical-free, biodegradable, vegetable oil-based,
> talc-free, unscented, dye-free, non-aerosol products; recyclable packaging

DECISION MAKING

1. How many of the products that you usually buy met some of the criteria above? How many of your favorite products fit none of the "green" criteria?
2. Many products that were at one time sold only in small health-food stores are now found in the supermarket. If you find that a "green" product you would like to try is not in your store, what can you do?
3. Compare two snack foods, one that contains no dyes, preservatives or chemicals and comes in recyclable or biodegradable packaging with a snack food that does not meet these criteria. Do a taste test. Which comes out ahead? Which one will you be more likely to buy in the future?

GOING FURTHER

Make your own nonpolluting window cleaning liquid. In a spray bottle, add 3 milliliters of a vegetable oil-based liquid soap and 45 milliliters of white vinegar to 500 milliliters of water. How well does this liquid clean a dirty window compared with a popular spray window cleaner? If the green solution does not do as good a job, can you live with it? Is it better than putting pollutants into your septic tank or sewer system?